WORLD OF SHAKESPEARE
SPORTS & PASTIMES

WORLD OF SHAKESPEARE

*

PLANTS
ANIMALS & MONSTERS
SPORTS & PASTIMES
GOD AND THE DEVIL

WORLD OF SHAKESPEARE:
SPORTS & PASTIMES

ALAN DENT

WITH A FOREWORD BY

DAME REBECCA WEST

TAPLINGER PUBLISHING CO., INC.
NEW YORK

First published in the United States in 1974 by
TAPLINGER PUBLISHING CO., INC.
New York, New York

Library of Congress Catalog Card Number: 72–13626

ISBN 0–8008–7365–3

FOREWORD

All his life long this critic, Alan Dent, has been a great reader
and a great admirer. The first is obviously an essential service
to civilization. There would be no great writers were there
not great readers, tireless souls who work on what they read
and survey the surface and mine the ore from the depths, and
spread the news of what they find, and so set off an endless
chain of writers and readers, readers and writers. As for great
admirers they go further and find more than great readers who
lack this second talent. For admiration implies warmth, a
capacity to glow at the recognition of the exceptionally
beautiful or wise; and happy is the great reader who has that
fuel in his engine, particularly when he goes on such a long
journey as the one taken by Alan Dent in this volume: all
through the works of Shakespeare, not a line missed, and out
at the other side.

How pleasant are all the interferences with one's normal
time-table which Alan Dent has been responsible for since he
sent me this little book! How enjoyable it has been for me to
find here full support for a theory about Shakespeare I formed
many years ago. I believe that Shakespeare's curious omni-
present absence, if one might call it so (his recorded appear-
ances all over the Tudor field and the emptiness of these
records) is due to the fact that great as the author might be, the
man himself was a bore, even an ace bore. I am delighted to
find that this critic goes all the way with me in this, groaning
over a number of passages, though I am bound to object that
one of the passages which makes him yawn loudest does not
seem to me boring at all. He would have the Recorder scene
in the third act of *Hamlet* excised as dreary nonsense, whereas
I see it as a sublime swipe of the brush which at one and the

same time indicates the inner workings of a human being and indicates the place he occupies in society. Surely this is a superb example of the combined shrewdness and rudeness of a privileged person, disgustingly rude, but not to be condemned out of hand because the persons who attend on the privileged are often such as deserve rudeness.

But for the rest Alan Dent and I are united in our weariness at the leaden quality of Shakespeare's lighter moments in his lesser plays. These terrible lapses in the greatest of writers are what engendered my theory. It is to be observed that Shakespeare is a bore only when he is writing of the joyful occasions when men and women gather together to have a good time by the exercise of sport and games and indulgence in wine and bawdry. Unlike the average man, he was at his best in crises; when the gods came to earth to wrestle for the souls of men, he was imaginatively there, and knew the right thing to say. But unlike the average man, he was no good at a party, in art, and, I feel sure, in life also.

'Such a good fellow,' they said of him, 'and not a bad writer. But don't ask him to your house. He will flog a feeble pun till it falls down dead, and his especially blue jokes would sink a galleon.' So Shakespeare stayed at home and wrote on and on, forced to concentrate on his work as if he were a honey-bee: laying up for us this store of lion's food, on which Alan Dent has banqueted all his life. Like the kind man he is, he shares the feast with us in this book.

REBECCA WEST

CONTENTS

A-Bed   9

Acting   10

Angling   12

Archery   13

Banqueting and Feasting   14

Bawdry   16

Bear-baiting   17

Betting and Wagering   18

Billiards   19

Boar-hunting   20

Bowls and Bowling   21

Brothel-haunting   23

Card-playing and Playing-cards   24

Children's Games   28

Cock-fighting   28

Dallying and Œillades   29

Dancing   31

Deviating   32

Dice, Hazard, Main   34

Duelling and Fencing   36

Eating and Drinking   36

Falconry   37

Games in General   38

Hunting and Coursing   42

Loving and Lusting   45

Music, Ho!   56

Music-making: 60

    Bagpipes   60

    Cymbals   61

    Drums   61

    Fifes   63

    Flutes   63

    Harps   64

    Hautboys   65

    Lutes   66

    Organ   67

    Pipes   68

    Psalteries   68

    Rebeck   68

    Recorders   69

    Sackbuts   70

    Tabors and Taborines   70

    Trumpets   71

    Viols and Viol-de-gamboys   73

    Virginals   73

Scrapping and Wrestling   74

Shovel-board   77

Contents

Songs and Singing: 79
    Airs 79
    Anthems 79
    Ballads 80
    Catches 81
    Ditties 82
    Hymns 84

Tunes 85
Swimming 86

Tennis 87

Walking 89
War-making 93

A-BED

This is a curious adverb of state or condition which Shakespeare uses half-a-dozen times and more, and in just as many different degrees of meaning.

When Duke Frederick misses his daughter Celia one morning, and asks what can have happened to her, an attendant Lord uses a phrase which can only mean that Celia went to bed, or was put to bed, in her normal way (*As You Like It*, II, ii, 5):

> The ladies, her attendants of her chamber,
> Saw her **a-bed**; and, in the morning early,
> They found the bed untreasured of their mistress.

She had risen early and run away with Rosalind to the Forest of Arden. Hence the whole comedy that follows.

When Sir Toby informs Sir Andrew that 'not to be **a-bed** after midnight is to be up betimes', he is being general rather than particular, though it takes some time for him to explain his breezy epigram to the foolish knight. Both sports and pastimes enter into the discussion (*Twelfth Night*, II, iii, 1).

When the King in his early-morning tirade before Agincourt has those two lines (*King Henry V*, IV, iii, 64):

> And gentlemen in England now **a-bed**
> Shall think themselves accurst they were not here; ...

he never fails to thrill one by conjuring up a marvellous vision of a million citizens of England about to rise for the day, and still blearily unaware of what is happening in France that same morning. The two lines have in them quite as much imagination as the fifty-odd that Chorus has to speak at the beginning of the same Act.

When Guiderius and Arviragus, the two boys in the care

of old Belisarius, longingly discuss the civilization which only their supposed father has known, they come away with lovely images in a passage (*Cymbeline*, III, iii, 29) where only the word 'a-bed' is cryptic and gives us pause:

> GUIDERIUS: ... Haply this life is best,
>   If quiet life be best; sweeter to you
>   That have a sharper known; well corresponding
>   With your stiff age; but unto us it is
>   A cell of ignorance; travelling **a-bed**; ...
> ARVIRAGUS: ... What should we speak of
>   When we are old as you? when we shall hear
>   The rain and wind beat dark December, how,
>   In this our pinching cave, shall we discourse
>   The freezing hours away? We have seen nothing ...

But what 'travelling a-bed' means, no editor of Shakespeare, from George Steevens downwards, seems able to tell us.

Elsewhere and everywhere else one is 'a-bed' for the purposes of sleep and rest, tossing and turning, procreation or parturition, or simply in being ill and hoping to get well again – or failing in that hope.

ACTING

This art can of course be regarded as sport or pastime only when it is amateur as distinct from professional. Thus the strolling players in *Hamlet* are not considered here since they acted for a living; whereas the troupe in *A Midsummer Night's Dream* gain admittance since they were by profession weaver, carpenter, joiner, tinker, tailor, and bellows-mender respectively.

The same may be said of the rather shapeless and ill-directed little inset drama of The Nine Worthies in the fifth act of *Love's Labour's Lost*. This is a nice muddle from the very beginning when the King of Navarre announces the cast in an undecided mixture of prose and verse (v, ii, 529):

> Here is like to be a good presence of Worthies.
> He [Armado] presents Hector of Troy; the swain
> [Costard the clown], Pompey the Greek; the parish curate,
> Alexander; Armado's page, Hercules; the pedant,
> Judas Maccabaeus:
> > And if these four Worthies in their first show thrive,
> > These four will change habits, and present the other five.

Why does young Shakespeare in this little pageant-play give us only five Worthies instead of nine? The original nine are usually supposed to be three pagans, three Jews, and three Christians. The usual choice is Hector, Alexander, and Julius Caesar for the pagans; Joshua, David, and Judas Maccabaeus for the Jews; and King Arthur, Charlemagne, and Godfrey of Bouillon for the worthy Christians. But why has the dramatist – in this interlude in what is usually reckoned to be his first play – given us an incomplete list of five Worthies including Pompey and Hercules who are not on the traditional list? Doubtless young Shakespeare was deliberately wrong in the matter, just as John Dryden a century later was impeccably correct:

> > Nine worthies were they called, of different rites,
> > Three Jews, three pagans, and three Christian Knights.

Hamlet's speech to the players (III, ii, I) is very well known, and most playgoers agree with his rounding upon the strolling troupe and telling them (not unlike a Granville-Barker of our own day) not to over-act, or over-shout, or over-gesticulate, and not to hold, as 'twere, a *distorting* mirror up to nature. But much less well-known – and well worth an occasional reading or even a performance – is W. S. Gilbert's satirical playlet, *Rosencrantz and Guildenstern* in which the First Player gives an indignant back-answer to Hamlet, putting him in his princely place:

Sir, we are beholden to you for your good counsels. But we would urge upon your consideration that we are accomplished players, who have spent many years in learning our profession; and we would venture to suggest that it would better befit your lordship to confine yourself to such matters as your lordship may be likely to understand. We, on our part, may have our own ideas as to the duties of heirs-apparent; but it would ill become us to air them before your lordship, who may be reasonably supposed to understand such matters more perfectly than your very humble servants.

Some may agree that this is a well-deserved rebuke, and a rebuke as just as it is eloquent.

ANGLING

Fishing with rod and line was one of the many games and sports which Cleopatra practised when Antony was away at his war-making. Quite early in the play she says to her handmaid Charmian (*Antony and Cleopatra*, II, v, 10):

> Give me mine **angle**,—we'll to the river: there,
> My music playing far off, I will betray
> Tawny-finn'd fishes; my bended hook shall pierce
> Their slimy jaws; and, as I draw them up,
> I'll think them every one an Antony,
> And say 'Ah, ha! y'are caught.'

Was this not love indeed?

Again, in *Much Ado About Nothing* (III, i, 26) when Beatrice is eavesdropping in 'the woodbine coverture', Ursula says to Hero:

> The pleasant'st **angling** is to see the fish
> Cut with her golden oars the silver stream,
> And greedily devour the treacherous bait:
> So **angle** we for Beatrice; . . .

[12]

And Edgar, pretending madness to Lear, Gloster and Kent, has his insane and eerie exclamation (*King Lear*, III, vi, 6): 'Frateretto calls me, and tells me Nero is an **angler** in the lake of darkness.'

But there is very little else to suggest that the man Shakespeare often went fishing in the River Avon in youth or in age. Unlike his near-contemporary Izaak Walton he might, from any evidence in his plays, be termed an incompleat angler.

But it is Cleopatra, continuing her conversation with Charmian (*Antony and Cleopatra*, II, v, 16), who deserves the last word on this sport and proceeds upwards from it to a sport nearer and dearer to her spacious heart:

> CHARMIAN: 'Twas merry when
> You wager'd on your **angling**; when your diver
> Did hang a salt-fish on his hook, which he
> With fervency drew up.
> CLEOPATRA: That time,—O times!—
> I laugh'd him out of patience; and that night
> I laugh'd him into patience: and next morn,
> Ere the ninth hour, I drunk him to his bed;
> Then put my tires and mantles on him, whilst
> I wore his sword Philippan.

ARCHERY

Archery is a mode of attack in time of war, but only a sport in time of peace. The only reference to it in the latter form is in a little scene in *Titus Andronicus* (IV, iii, 2), where Titus and his brother Marcus and his young son Lucius bring in bows and arrows, and the father says to his son:

> Sir boy, now let me see your **archery**;
> Look ye draw home enough, and 'tis there straight.

[13]

This bout of archery happens in a public place in Rome. And the archers take aim with various gods in mind (IV, iii, 52):

> You are a good **archer**, Marcus;
> *Ad Jovem*, that's for you:—here, *Ad Apollinem*:—
> *Ad Martem*, that's for myself:—
> Here, boy, *To Pallas*:—here, *To Mercury*:—
> *To Saturn*, Caius, not to Saturnine;
> You were as good to shoot against the wind.—
> To it, boy!—Marcus, loose when I bid.—
> Of my word, I have written to effect;
> There's not a god left unsolicited.

But to Shakespeare himself, as poet and playwright, Cupid would appear to have been the bowman who gave him most pleasure and stirred his fancy most.

See also BOWLS AND BOWLING.

BANQUETING AND FEASTING

Whereas meals three or four times daily are ordinary things that keep one alive, banquets are – in the purest sense of that overworked word – extraordinary. They are, or should be, life at its uppermost level, so far as eating goes. They are feasting-in-style. They therefore qualify for entry into life's sports and pastimes.

In *King Henry V* the Archbishop of Canterbury deplores the irresponsible behaviour of Prince Hal (I, i, 55):

> His companies unletter'd, rude, and shallow;
> His hours fill'd up with riots, **banquets**, sports; . . .

We have scarcely met Antony and his Cleopatra for the first time when Enobarbus and the queen's attendants – including her two handmaids, her eunuch, and her soothsayer – appear

to be having a banquet on their own account (*Antony and Cleopatra*, I, ii, 11).
Enobarbus speaks:

> Bring in the **banquet** quickly; wine enough
> Cleopatra's health to drink.

In *King Henry VI, Part One* (II, i, 11), Talbot wants to storm the unprepared enemy:

> This happy night the Frenchmen are secure,
> Having all day coursed and **banqueted**:
> Embrace we, then, this opportunity, . . .

And Old Capulet in *Romeo and Juliet* uses that rare figure of speech, inverted irony, when he tries to coax some gate-crashing Montagues to stay on at his party (I, v, 123):

> Nay, gentlemen, prepare not to be gone;
> We have a trifling foolish **banquet** towards.

These and other banquets – whether in London or Alexandria, Orleans or Verona – were obviously a great success. But the best-known of all, the one given by the Macbeths at Forres, was doomed to failure, almost from the start, by the arrival of the bloody spectre of the newly-murdered Banquo, shaking his gory locks. This is not called a banquet by anyone who went to it, alive or dead. It is a banquet only in the stage-direction at the beginning of Act III Scene iv – '**Banquet** prepared.'

As for feasting, the little speech of the Herald in *Othello* (II, ii) – it is the whole scene and no one else has a word – might serve almost as a motto for this whole book. It is a proclamation which would also serve for any young actor to make his mark in, if he has a good proclaiming voice. Yet in the theatre it is stupidly and almost invariably cut:

It is Othello's pleasure, our noble and valiant general, that, upon certain tidings now arrived, importing the mere perdition of the

Turkish fleet, every man put himself into triumph; some to dance, some to make bonfires, each man to what sport and revels his addiction leads him: for, besides these beneficial news, it is the celebration of his nuptial:—so much was his pleasure should be proclaim'd. All offices are open; and there is full liberty of **feasting** from this present hour of five till the bell have told eleven. Heaven bless the isle of Cyprus and our noble general Othello!

BAWDRY

To talk bawdry, or even to live in it, cannot strictly be called either a sport or a pastime, since it simply signifies indulgence in lewd language or lewd practices. But Shakespeare uses the word only three times – as distinct from 'bawd' (which he uses unendingly) – and on each of these three occasions the malpractice could conceivably pass muster as a sport.

Thus, Touchstone says to Audrey, the country wench he proposes to marry (*As You Like It*, III, iii, 90):

Come, sweet Audrey:
We must be married, or we must live in **bawdry.**

Thus, Hamlet rebukes Polonius for his interruption of the First Player (*Hamlet*, II, ii, 507): 'Prithee, say on:—he's for a jig or a tale of **bawdry**, or he sleeps:—say on: come to Hecuba.'

And thus, in *The Winter's Tale*, the Clown's Servant, who is almost always severely cut when the play is acted. This unexplained character called 'Servant' is not even in the list of the dramatis personae. His function is to announce the arrival of Autolycus, and he does so in three patches of vigorous prose within the same little scene (IV, iii, 191). The second of these, a blue rather than a purple patch, runs thus:

He hath songs for man, or woman, of all sizes, no milliner can so fit his customers with gloves: he has the prettiest love-songs for maids; so without **bawdry**, which is strange; with such delicate budens [= delightful refrains] of 'dildos' and 'fadings', 'jump her and thump her'; and where some stretch-mouth'd rascal would, as it were, mean mischief, and break a foul jape into the matter, he makes the maid to answer, 'Whoop, do me no harm, good man'; puts him off, slights him, with 'Whoop, do me no harm, good man'.

Cuttable certainly, though the obvious references to old ballads must fascinate the folklorist.

BEAR-BAITING

The references in *The Merry Wives of Windsor* to dancing and performing bears – including Sackerson, which was a famous Elizabethan bear apparently called after its master, a bear-trainer – do not concern the so-called sport of setting dogs to attack a bear chained to a stake.

This savage form of fun is referred to only in *The Winter's Tale* and *Twelfth Night*. In the one the Clown says of Autolycus the peddling rogue (iv, ii, 101): 'He haunts wakes, fairs, and **bear-baitings**.' And in the other the foolish knight, Sir Andrew Aguecheek, remarks with a delicious melancholy (i, iii, 90): 'I would I had bestow'd that time in the tongues that I have in fencing, dancing and **bear-baiting**. O, had I but follow'd the arts!'

BETTING AND WAGERING

Osric in *Hamlet* goes on so about the betting and wagering that is to accompany Hamlet's duel with Laertes (v, ii, 146) that we are always glad that in the theatre his part is liberally slashed by his director:

OSRIC: The king, sir, hath **wager'd** with him six Barbary horses: against the which he has impawned, as I take it, six French rapiers and poniards, with their assigns, as girdle, hanger, and so: three of the carriages, in faith, are very dear to fancy, very responsive to the hilts, most delicate carriages, and of very liberal conceit.

HAMLET: What call you the carriages? . . .

OSRIC: The carriages, sir, are the hangers.

HAMLET: The phrase would be more germane to the matter, if we could carry a cannon by our sides: I would it might be hangers till then. But, on: six Barbary horses against six French swords, their assigns, and three liberal-conceited carriages; that's the French **bet** against the Danish . . .

And so the rigmarole goes on, both before and after, in the text if not in the theatre, where we know to expect very soon the comparatively significant speech to Horatio: 'We defy augury: . . . the readiness is all: . . .'

Nym with Pistol in *King Henry V* (II, i, 97) is at least brief about his bet when he says: 'You'll pay me the eight shillings I won of you at **betting?**' and gets the answer: 'Base is the slave that pays.' However, only ten lines later Nym repeats his demand, and receives from Pistol at least a promise: 'A noble shalt thou have, and present pay.'

Of countless other wagerers in the plays only Emilia and Iachimo need to be singled out. The first for her protestation to Othello about her mistress's innocence (IV, ii, 12):

> I durst, my lord, to **wager** she is honest,
> Lay down my soul at **stake**: if you think other,
> Remove your thought,—it doth abuse your bosom.

[18]

And Iachimo in *Cymbeline* (I, vi, 15) utters this exquisitely phrased speech to himself while watching Imogen read the letter he has brought to her from her trusting husband:

> All of her that is out door most rich!
> If she be furnisht with a mind so rare,
> She is alone the Arabian bird; and I
> Have lost the **wager**. Boldness be my friend!
> Arm me, audacity, from head to foot!
> Or, like the Parthian, I shall flying fight;
> Rather, directly fly.

BILLIARDS

The only mention in the whole of Shakespeare is to an actual match that is never played, merely suggested. This is discussed by Cleopatra and her maids and her eunuch Mardian, while the Queen is trying to beguile the weary and aching time of Antony's absence in Rome (II, v, 3):

CLEOPATRA: Let it alone; let's to **billiards**:
                                    come, Charmian.
CHARMIAN: My arm is sore; best play with Mardian.
CLEOPATRA: As well a woman with an eunuch play'd,
    As with a woman.—Come, you'll play with me, sir?
MARDIAN: As well as I can, madam.
CLEOPATRA: And when good will is show'd, though't come too
    short,
    The actor may plead pardon. I'll none now:—
    Give me mine angle,—we'll to the river: ...

A delicately indelicate bit of by-play around a game of billiards that never even began.

BOAR-HUNTING

There are in Shakespeare enough references to the wild boar to convince us that this was at least as familiar a sight to the Elizabethan as the hare or the hedgehog are to us today.

Petruchio in *The Taming of the Shrew* (I, ii, 200) describes his own dauntless spirit:

> Have I not heard the sea, puff'd up with winds,
> Rage like an angry **boar** chafèd with sweat?

Aaron the Moor, in *Titus Andronicus* (IV, ii, 137) describes his own black rage in similar terms:

> ... but if you brave the Moor,
> The chafèd **boar,** the mountain lioness,
> The ocean swells not so as Aaron storms.

A Senator tells Timon in *Timon of Athens* (v, i, 164) of an invader who is boar-like, and as arrogant as his name:

> ... so soon we shall drive back
> Of Alcibiades th'approaches wild;
> Who, like a **boar** too savage, doth root up
> His country's peace.

In *As You Like It* (I, iii, 114) Rosalind, dressing up as the boy Ganymede to go into the Forest of Arden, is fully prepared for an encounter with a wild boar at least:

> A gallant curtle-axe upon my thigh,
> A **boar-spear** in my hand; ...

And it is in the Boar's-Head tavern in Eastcheap, at the rich human heart of *King Henry IV, Part Two* (II, iv, 228), that Doll Tearsheet has an ironic description of her old fondling fat knight:

Thou whoreson little tidy Bartholomew **boar-pig**, when wilt thou leave fighting o' days and foining o' nights, and begin to patch up thine old body for heaven?

But turning away from the plays to the poems, it is an actual and particular wild-boar that might be called the only other character over and above the eponymous pair in *Venus and Adonis*. This great, voluptuous, under-read and under-estimated poem is almost as much about the shepherd Adonis chasing the wild-boar as about the goddess Venus chasing young Adonis.

In its very beginning (lines 1–4) the theme is stated almost before 'sick-thoughted' Venus herself appears:

> Even as the sun with purple-colour'd face
> Has ta'en his last leave of the weeping morn,
> Rose-cheek'd Adonis hied him to the chase;
> Hunting he lov'd, but love he laugh'd to scorn: ...

Venus tells the youth she will do all she can 'to make thee hate the hunting of the **boar**' (line 711). And it is Venus and not Adonis who describes the beast as 'this foul, grim, and urchin-snouted **boar**' (line 1105).

In the end – need one tell non-readers of this discursive epic? – it is the wild boar, and not Venus, that gets Adonis at the conclusion of the chase—which is the conclusion of the poem.

BOWLS AND BOWLING

In the Duke of York's garden at Langley, King Richard II's Queen declines a game of bowls (*King Richard II*, III, iv, 1):

> QUEEN: What sport shall we devise here in this garden,
>   To drive away the heavy thought of care?
> LADY: Madam, we'll play at **bowls**.

> QUEEN: 'Twill make me think the world is full of rubs,
> And that my fortune runs against the bias.

Menenius in *Coriolanus* (v, ii, 19), insisting to a Sentinel on his loyalty to his General, has a figurative reference to the same game:

> ... nay, sometimes,
> Like to a **bowl** upon a subtle ground,
> I have tumbled past the throw; and in his praise
> Have almost stampt the leasing: therefore, fellow,
> I must have leave to pass.

But throughout a whole scene of *Love's Labour's Lost* (IV, i,) a sport is in progress and it is never really clear whether the reference is to a game of bowls or a bout of archery. It is a scene in artificial language which strains the patience even of that patient scholar, Granville-Barker, who devotes one of his celebrated *Prefaces to Shakespeare* – the very first of them – to this play itself, and several pages to this particularly difficult scene. This is an analysis in which he more than once comes near to losing his critical temper. The scene – not a particularly short one either – is 'horribly stuffed' with archaic words and phrases, obscure topical jokes, maddening puns on 'suitors' and 'shooters'. It is a scene which achieves a non-archaic significance only in the very last line of all, when Costard suddenly hits upon the right modern word for Don Armado's page, Moth:

> And his page o' t'other side, that handful of wit!
> Ah, heavens, it is a most pathetical nit!

Dr Caroline Spurgeon, the supreme authority on Shakespearean images, has been able to count no fewer than nineteen images drawn from the game of bowls, and concludes – with something less than her usual caution – that it was the game that Shakespeare himself 'played and loved best'.

BROTHEL-HAUNTING

Laertes, brother of Ophelia and son of Polonius, was suspected of such a sport when he went back to Paris, and in a charmingly natural little scene in *Hamlet* (a scene which is too often cut in stage-performances) the old man sends his servant Reynaldo to find out how his son is behaving or misbehaving himself in that adventurous city (II, i, 19):

> ... there put on him
> What forgeries you please; marry, none so rank
> As may dishonour him; take heed of that;
> But, sir, such wanton, wild, and usual slips
> As are companions noted and most known
> To youth and liberty.
> REYNALDO: As gaming, my lord.
> POLONIUS: Ay, or drinking, fencing, swearing,
>   Quarrelling, drabbing [= whoring]:—you may go
>   so far.

Reynaldo must bring all such reports back with him to Elsinore (II, i, 59):

> ... or perchance,
> 'I saw him enter such a house of sale,'—
> Videlicet, a **brothel**, or so forth.

Marina in *Pericles* miraculously keeps her virgin virtue though immured for a time in exactly 'such a house of sale'. This strange wandering play has one pretty patch of dialogue (IV, ii 139) between a bawd, Boult (described as a 'Servant of a Pander' – which is surely the lowest of the low, in the matter of professions) and Marina herself, who emerges, somehow, uncontaminated:

BAWD: Boult, spend thou that in the town: report what a sojourner we have; you'll lose nothing by custom. When Nature framed this

[23]

piece, she meant thee a good turn; therefore say what a paragon she is, and thou hast the harvest out of thine own report.

BOULT: I warrant you, mistress, thunder shall not so awake the beds of eels as my giving out her beauty stirs up the lewdly-inclined. I'll bring home some to-night.

BAWD: Come your ways, follow me.

MARINA: If fires be hot, knives sharp, or waters deep,
Untied I still my virgin knot will keep.
Diana, aid my purpose!

BAWD: What have we to do with Diana?

Edgar in *King Lear*, on the other hand, talks himself out of such resorts, though he sounds at times rather like a regular customer (III, iv, 95):

Let not the creaking of shoes nor the rustling of silks
betray thy poor heart to woman; keep thy foot out
of **brothels**, thy hand out of plackets, . . .

Oddly enough the frequently-visited brothel in *Measure for Measure* is never called 'brothel' *tout court*, though the simple constable whose name is Elbow describes it (II, i, 65) as 'a hot-house, which, I think is, a very ill house too'. Moreover its manageress is called Mistress Overdone and her servant Pompey Bum, while Claudio and Lucio are among the establishment's many regular customers, its haunters. Disorderly, undoubtedly!

CARD-PLAYING AND PLAYING-CARDS

That major and senior drama-critic and superb Shakespearean scholar, Mr Ivor Brown, manifests his great interest in these notebooks by sending me a valuable note concerning Shakespeare and card-games. Where we refer to a 'pack' of cards, Shakespeare (he tells me) tends to use the much older word 'deck'; a usage which still survives in America. Thus Gloster at the end of the *Third Part of King Henry VI* has an intricate image which comes a shade clearer if we know this (v, i, 42–46):

> Alas, that Warwick had no more forecast,
> But, whiles he thought to steal the single ten,
> The king was slily fingered from the **deck**!
> You left poor Henry at the bishop's palace,
> And, ten to one, you'll meet him in the Tower.

Where Tranio in *The Taming of the Shrew* has a figurative reference to a card-game (ii, 1, 399–400):

> A vengeance on your crafty withered hide!
> Yet I have faced it with a **card of ten**
> 'Tis in my head to do my master good . . .

the New Penguin edition has a note that 'to outface with a card of ten' was a proverbial phrase for bluffing. But the reference may just possibly be to the half-forgotten card-game of one's childhood called Catch the Ten.

Then again, the French Dauphin in *King John* (v, ii, 105–108) has a figurative reference to playing-cards when he is seeking to win renown 'even in the jaws of danger and of death'. He says to the papal legate, Pandulph:

> Have I not here the best cards for the game
> To win this easy match, played for a crown?
> And shall I now give o'er the yielded set?
> No, no on my soul, it never shall be said.

Antony describes his Queen's seeming treachery to his faithful servant Eros in terms of cards (iv, xiv, 19–23):

> . . . She, Eros has
> Packed cards with Caesar, and false-play'd my glory
> Unto an enemy's triumph,
> Nay, weep not, gentle Eros, there is left us
> Ourselves to end ourselves.

And Aaron in *Titus Andronicus* (v, 1, 98–101) gloats over his own villainy and that of his two sons who have raped and mutilated Lavinia:

> Indeed, I was their tutor to instruct them;
> That codding (= eager) spirit had they from their mother,
> As sure a card as ever won the set;
> That bloody mind I think they learned of me . . .

Lysander has a footling pleasantry on the death of Pyramus in the play-scene in *The Dream* (v, 1, 298): – 'Less than an **ace**, man; for he is dead, he is nothing.' And Don Adriano de Armado bandies words drawn from playing-cards with Moth, his page in *Love's Labour's Lost* (1, ii, 49–53):

MOTH: I am sure you know how much the gross sum of **deuce ace** amounts to.
ARMADO: It doth amount to one more than two.
MOTH: Which the base vulgar do call three.
ARMADO: True.

That most sinister of all the playing-cards known as The Joker is not mentioned anywhere in Shakespeare, and indeed is not – according to the Oxford Dictionary – mentioned anywhere as a playing-card until as late as the year 1885. In play it 'counts usually as a trump, and sometimes the highest trump' but it would appear to be used only in certain gambling games, notably in the game of Poker (1848), the American variant of the English game of Brag (1734).

The Joker is depicted usually, but not always, as a jester with a diabolical grin, either squatting with knees wide apart or standing up, and usually with a bauble in one hand and an indeterminate ace-card in the other. 'The eye of childhood – or that of this compiler at least – feared him as a kind of painted devil (to adapt the phrase of Lady Macbeth).' And it is by no means irrelevant to recall, in one's Scottish infancy, that old women usually referred to playing-cards as Devil's Cards (and may do so still). One recalls also that in a first schoolroom reading of *Twelfth Night* – and indeed in every subsequent reading or viewing of that same play – one gets a curious sensation of a little jester turned evil, or of a little devil turned jester leaping uncannily through the lines whether Feste the clown sings or merely speaks them (IV, 2, 121):

> I am gone, sir, and anon, sir,
> I'll be with you again—
> In a trice, like to the old Vice,
> Your need to sustain.
> Who with dagger of lath, in his rage and his wrath,
> Cries Ah ha! to the devil;
> Like a mad lad – Pare thy nails, dad?
> Adieu, goodman devil!

It is by no means an outstanding lyric, its rhyme on 'devil' is no rhyme at all, not even an assonance, but a mere repetition. It is all undoubtedly inconsequent; but it is also faintly devilish.

The New Penguin edition of the play – meticulously edited by Professor M. M. Mahood – tells us that the Vice was a character who defied the devil in the early Tudor interludes which developed from the Morality plays, and that he was one ancestor of the Elizabethan stage fool. He also explains the curious 'Pare thy nails, dad?' with a reference to *Henry V* (IV, iv, 69–70) which suggests that the Vice in the old plays used to try to pare the Devil's long nails. This edition, which is particularly sound on the musical settings, declares that no early music has survived for 'I am gone, sir', this diabolical little ditty.

CHILDREN'S GAMES

Hide-and-seek, perhaps the earliest of children's games, does not seem to exist in Shakespeare, not at least under that apellation – which the *Oxford English Dictionary* declares to be no earlier than 1672. On the other hand, blindman's buff has the honour to be mentioned by Hamlet himself, under the title of 'hoodman-blind', and in the Closet Scene with his mother (*Hamlet*, III, iv, 77):

> What devil was't
> That thus hath cozen'd you at **hoodman-blind**? . . .
> O shame! where is thy blush?

A child's hoop, and the hoop-iron with which it is trundled, would seem to have been among the possessions of the little Prince Mamillius in *The Winter's Tale*; or so at least this writer thought until he looked for confirmation in the Mamillius scenes in the play. There is no mention whatever of any hoop or hoop-iron. Was there perhaps some picture of little Mamillius with this toy, the hoop in one hand, the hoop-iron in the other? Possibly, an early, long-lost photograph of Ellen Terry in the part?

But the recollection is as vague as a dream and, no less unconfirmable. It is much more certain that Ellen Terry played Mamillius in her infancy (with Mr and Mrs Charles Kean) and that in her old age she included the touching little part prominently in her lecture, 'The Children in Shakespeare's Plays'.

COCK-FIGHTING

This is a very ancient sport which used to be much practised in England (and which, though illegal, is practised still if we take note of hole-and-corner mentions in the public press). It is all the odder, therefore, that references to it are few and rare in Shakespeare, and usually oblique.

That vain and grotesque prince, Cloten, has a sidelong reference in *Cymbeline* (ii, i, 18) when he says:

> I had rather not be so noble as I am; they dare not
> fight with me, because of the queen my mother: every
> Jack-slave hath his bellyful of fighting, and I
> must go up and down like a **cock** that nobody can match.

Also the Chorus in *King Henry V* (Prologue to Act i, lines 11–12) very obviously has in mind the little arena where cocks did – and do – their fighting when he refers to the inadequacy of the theatre to stage a human battle:

> . . . can this **cockpit** hold
> The vasty fields of France?

DALLYING AND ŒILLADES

In *Venus and Adonis* (lines 105–8) the goddess of love tells her wayward Adonis how his predecessor Mars, the god of war

> . . . for my sake hath learnt to sport and dance,
> To toy, to wanton, **dally**, smile, and jest;
> Scorning his churlish drum and ensign red,
> Making my arms his field, his tent my bed.

In *King Henry VI, Part One*, the king tells his uncle that he prefers to improve his mind rather than tempt his body (v, i, 22):

> And fitter is my study and my books
> Than wanton **dalliance** with a paramour. . . .

In *King Richard III* (iii, vii, 74) Buckingham describes Gloucester with unconscious irony:

> Not **dallying** with a brace of courtesans,
> But meditating with two deep divines;
> Not sleeping, to engross his idle body,
> But praying, to enrich his watchful soul:
> Happy were England, would this virtuous prince
> Take on himself the sovereignty thereof;
> But sure I fear we shall not win him to it.

Any other word for not-very-deep love-making is rare indeed in Shakespeare. Both 'flirt' and 'coquette' are eighteenth-century, whereas the silly 'spooning' is Edwardian and the coarse 'necking' belongs to the last decade or so. But 'flirt' is found in a compound form in *Romeo and Juliet* (II, iii, 156) when the Nurse says of Mercutio: 'Scurvy knave! I am none of his flirt-gills' and merely means 'fast girls'.

However, there is one strange word for a coquettish or calculating glance that is far from shallow, in fact as deep as it sounds. It is directly French in origin and it occurs twice in Shakespeare.

The first scene is between Falstaff and Pistol in *The Merry Wives of Windsor* (I, iii, 56), where the former says he has written a letter to Mrs Page,

> ... who even now gave me good eyes too,
> examined my parts with most judicious **œillades**; sometimes
> the beam of her view gilded my foot, sometimes my
> portly belly.
> PISTOL: Then did the sun on dunghill shine.

The second scene is in *King Lear* between Cornwall's widow, Regan, and the despicable Oswald who is Goneril's serving-man (and willing to serve anyone else who may come his way) (IV, v, 23):

> REGAN: I know your lady does not love her husband;
> I am sure of that: and at her late being here
> She gave strange **œillades** and most speaking looks
> To noble Edmund. I know you are of her bosom.
> OSWALD: Ay, madam.

REGAN: I speak in understanding; you are, I know't:
    Therefore I do advise you, take this note:
    My lord is dead; Edmund and I have talk'd;
    And more convenient is he for my hand
    Than for your lady's:—you may gather more. . . .

Much virtue – and vice – in Oswald's laconic 'Ay, madam'.

But why one scene should make us laugh while the other scene makes us shudder is just part of the dramatic mystery of things.

DANCING

There is set-dancing in several of the plays – including Capulet's ball in *Romeo and Juliet*, the *bal masqué* in *Much Ado About Nothing*, and a rough dance of shepherds in *The Winter's Tale* described beforehand by the garrulous Second Clown (IV, iii, 326):

Master, there is three carters, three shepherds, three neat-herds, three swine-herds, that have made themselves all men of hair,—they call themselves Saltiers: and they have a **dance** which the wenches say is a gallimaufry of gambols, because they are not in't; but they themselves are o' the mind,—if it be not too rough for some that know little but bowling,— it will please plentifully.

There is, too, the incessant tripping of fairies in *A Midsummer Night's Dream* (not absolutely always to Mendelssohn, but sometimes to English folk-tunes—which makes a pleasant change).

Individual dances also get frequent mention. For example, in *King Henry V* (III, v, 32) the Duke of Bourbon echoes the Dauphin who has been chiding Frenchwomen for running after English soldiery:

        They bid us to the English dancing-schools,
        And teach **lavoltas** high and swift **corantos**;
        Saying our grace is only in our heels,
        And that we are most lofty runaways.

And Sir Toby teases Sir Andrew about his light-foot accomplishment and ends a scene by making him exit dancing like giddy goat, in *Twelfth Night* (I, iii, 116):

SIR TOBY: What is thy excellence in a **galliard**, knight?

SIR ANDREW: Faith, I can cut a caper. . . .

SIR TOBY: Wherefore are these things hid? wherefore have these gifts a curtain before 'em? . . . why dost thou not go to church in a **galliard**, and come home in a **coranto**?

But the obscurest reference of all – and it is in the same play – is to the **pavane**, a stately dance of the sixteenth century. This is in a passage where Sir Toby describes someone disparagingly (v, i 197): 'Then he's a rogue, and a *passy-measures pavin*'. It is a phrase which is even beyond the scholars, though Editor Ridley has a good, laboured try: 'The pavin (pavane) was a slow dance, one variety of which was "passy-measures" (passamezzo); and the "strains" of it were of eight bars each.' This seems to us the very ecstasy of pedantry.

DEVIATING

Post-Freudian scholarship has, rather surprisingly, been reticent in the matter of flashlighting certain excesses in friendship in the works of Shakespeare. For example, that between Rosalind and Celia in *As You Like It*, those heavenly cousins of whom the courtier, Monsieur Le Beau, says – for what it is worth – that their loves were 'dearer than the natural bond of sisters' (I, ii, 267). Or even that between Cassio and Iago in *Othello*, though the wicked fantasy and invention of the latter's story (about Cassio's sleep-talking) is a double-dyed device to torment Othello's rage at his wife and her imagined duplicity (III, iii, 413). It is perhaps the most diabolical lie in the whole of drama.

Yet again when Hero says of her cousin Beatrice in *Much Ado About Nothing* (III, i, 54):

> ... she cannot love,
> Nor take no shape nor project of affection,
> She is so self-endear'd. ...

she does not really imply that her merry cousin is self-sufficient to the point of eternal spinsterdom. And it would be a very daring and very young scholar who tried to maintain that Macbeth is revealing that onanism is among his many misdemeanours when he declares (III, iv, 142):

> ... My strange and self-abuse
> Is the initiate fear, that wants hard use: ...

What Macbeth really means here is quite beside the point. But it is not that! The play's most recent editor, Mr G. K. Hunter of the New Penguin Shakespeare, translates it thus: 'My strange self-deception (seeing Banquo's ghost) is only due to the terror of the beginner who lacks toughening experience.' The mutual passion between the Grecian captains, Achilles and Patrochus, is declared and explicit in *Troilus and Cressida*.

Reverting to Rosalind and Celia, we asked a young student of the play who had been deep in its study whether he found in it any reference to any kind of 'permissive' behaviour. He immediately quoted Celia's lines to her own father about her friendship with Rosalind (I, iii, 69):

> ... if she be a traitor,
> Why, so am I; we still have slept together,
> Rose at an instant, learn'd, play'd, ate together;
> And wheresoe'er we went, like Juno's swans,
> Still we went coupled and inseparable.

Asked to explain, this modern student said, without a smirk or seeming smartness: 'Well, they slept together – she says so herself!'

This is the age we live in, and the way it thinks and reads. *C'est plus fort que moi!*

Deviating to my own childhood, let me recall here, across the many years, the English class-room in my Scottish school, and the consternation I once caused there by reading aloud a passage in *As You Like It* from my one-volume Shakespeare where the rest of the class used an edition for schools. The sensation – which took the form of giggling from the boys and gasps from the girls – came about when I had the luck to read part of the scene between Rosalind and Celia speculating on the identity of the poet – Orlando, of course – who had been hanging his verses on the trees of the Forest of Arden (III, 2, 191–198):

ROSALIND: I prithee tell me who is it quickly, and speak apace. I would thou couldst stammer, that thou mightst pour this concealed man out of thy mouth as wine comes out of a narrow-mouthed bottle: either too much at once, or none at all. I prithee take the cork out of thy mouth, that I may drink thy tidings.
CELIA: So you may put a man in your belly.

Our English master glared, seized my book to make quite certain I was reading what was printed, and thereafter sent a note to my poor father begging him to buy me the same 'school edition' used by the rest of the twelve-year-olds and thus to spare him the embarrassment of explanation. It was my first lesson in the dangers of non-conformity.

DICE, HAZARD, MAIN

Shakespeare's direct references to the actual game of dice are few, but two of them are most vivid and important. One is that of Edgar in *King Lear* (III, iv, 90) who in his self-derogation as the vagabond madman, Poor Tom, declares himself to have been

> . . . one that slept in the contriving of lust,
> and waked to do it: wine loved I deeply,

> **dice** dearly; and in woman out-paramour'd
> the Turk: ...

The other is that of Chorus in *KingHenry V*(IV, Prologue,17):

> Proud of their numbers, and secure in soul,
> The confident and over-lusty French
> Do the low-rated English play at **dice**;
> And chide the cripple tardy-gaited night,
> Who, like a foul and ugly witch, doth limp
> So tediously away.

Shortly afterwards, when the Battle of Agincourt has turned in favour of the English, the Dauphin of France has a reference to this same sporting interlude (IV, v, 7):

> O pèrdurable shame!—let's stab ourselves.
> Be these the wretches that we played at **dice** for?

For this arresting piece of information – as for much else in the English historical plays – Shakespeare went straight to the old *Chronicles* of Raphael Holinshed.

> The Frenchmen in the meane while, as thoughe
> they had bin sure of victory, made great
> triumphe, for the captaines had determined before how
> to divide the spoile, and the souldiours the night
> before had plaid the englishemen at dice.

Was there ever so *obliged* a writer as Shakespeare?

Both 'hazard' and 'main' are words with a dozen different meanings even as nouns. But the oldest significance of 'hazard' is 'a game at dice in which the chances are complicated by a number of arbitrary rules'; and in one of its earliest uses (1575) a 'main' was in the game of hazard, 'a number (from five to nine inclusive) called by the "caster" before the dice are thrown'.

There is a reference to both, admittedly in the figurative sense, in *King Henry IV, Part One* (IV, i, 45) where Hotspur says:

[35]

> ... were it good
> To set the exact wealth of all our states
> All at one cast? to set so rich a **main**
> On the nice **hazard** of one doubtful hour?
> It were not good; ...

DUELLING AND FENCING

There is a brief but loaded summary of the whole art of fencing in *Twelfth Night* (III, iv, 276) where Sir Toby teases Sir Andrew about the prowess of Sebastian who has challenged him to a duel:

> Why, man, he's a very devil; I have not seen such
> a firago. I had a pass with him, rapier, scabbard,
> and all, and he gives me the stuck-in with such a
> mortal motion, that it is inevitable; and on the answer,
> he pays you as surely as your feet hit the ground
> they step on: they say he has been **fencer** to the
> Sophy [the Shah of Persia].

And Sir Andrew answers: 'Pox on't, I'll not meddle with him.'

There are some young men in the plays who seem to live entirely *for* fencing and duelling like Tybalt in *Romeo and Juliet*, or who live entirely *by* it like Osric in *Hamlet*. You might call them young blades rather than young men.

EATING AND DRINKING

Neither severally nor in combination do these two necessities of life constitute either a sport or a pastime. But there are at least two irresistible instances in the plays when they are considered together as the be-all and end-all of existence.

One is in *Twelfth Night* (II, iii, 9) where Sir Toby asks the question: 'Does not our life consist of the four elements?' and Sir Andrew supplies the characteristic answer: 'Faith, so they say; but, I think, it rather consists of **eating and drinking.**'

The other is in *Measure for Measure* (III, ii, 102), where the Duke, disguised as a friar, says to the unrepentant rake Lucio that lechery is too general a vice, and gets the answer: 'Yes, in good sooth, the vice is of a great kindred; it is well allied; but it is impossible to extirp it quite, friar, till **eating and drinking** be put down.'

FALCONRY

One has to know a little about falconry if one is fully to understand some of the best-known plays. Indeed, the author quite obviously presupposes much knowledge of this so-called sport in his contemporary audiences.

Hamlet welcomes the Players to Elsinore warmly and even excitedly (*Hamlet*, II, ii, 435):

HAMLET: Masters, you are all welcome. We'll e'en to't like French **falconers,** fly at any thing we see: we'll have a speech straight: come, give us a taste of your quality; come, a passionate speech.
FIRST PLAYER: What speech, my good lord?

This is clear and fine and urgent – all but that odd remark about French falconers. And it is boring to have to learn, or be told, that English falconers let some smaller bird fly into the air before sending off the falcon in pursuit of it, whereas the French falconers let off the falcon trusting it to aim at any bird within its line, and who can blame them?

When Juliet on her balcony tries to recall Romeo (*Romeo and Juliet*, II, i, 201):

> Hist! Romeo, hist!—O, for a **falconer's** voice,
> To lure this tassel-gentle back again!

she implies that she is already practised in the ancient art, 'the sport of kings', since at least four words in her last sentence of twelve has its special falconry sense – 'falconry', 'lure', 'tassel' (for 'tiercel'), and 'gentle'.

It is useful to have a glimmer of the meaning of these and a few other falconry words – that a 'tiercel' is a male falcon which is, surprisingly, only about a third of the size of the female falcon; that a 'haggard' is a wild female hawk caught when in her adult plumage; that a 'peregrine' hawk or falcon is a wandering bird of either sex; that a 'lure' is a bait to which a bird-wing or a tuft of feathers has been tied; that a 'jess' is a short strap of leather or silk fastened round each leg of a hawk used in falconry.

Facilities for *hawking* are among the pleasures offered by the Lord to poor bamboozled Christopher Sly in *The Taming of the Shrew* (Induction ii, 45–60):

> Dost thou love **hawking**? thou hast hawks will soar
> Above the morning lark.

GAMES IN GENERAL

It is true that Shakespeare mentions remarkably few games of any sort. But it would be wrong to conclude that he was no playboy, by which one means gamesman. The fact is that the greater part of the games we know are later in date than Elizabethan or Jacobean times. Chess, dice, and playing-cards are, of course, much older. But of the card-games still played – and some no longer played—nearly all are of later date than 1616, the year when Shakespeare died.

There is no record of solitaire (played with marbles on a special board) before 1746, or of any of the innumerable forms of patience, the solo card-game, before 1816. Accounts of whist are not traceable before 1663, and its predecessor which was spelt 'whisk' was only twenty years older and is therefore not found in Shakespeare. Neither, rather surprisingly, is backgammon. Still more surprising is the absence of skittles (which did not seem to exist under that name before 1634) and of its predecessor called 'ninepins' which is mentioned by other writers as early at 1580.

Cribbage does not appear to have existed before 1630, and ombre and loo (and the latter's predecessor 'lanterloo' and 'langtriloo') seem first to have been played by Restoration ladies – as we know from their stage-counterparts.

The easiest and apparently the most primitive of all the card-games, snap or snip-snap-snorum, goes no farther back than the middle of the eighteenth century.

Shakespeare's references to actual card-games are therefore few and indeterminate. When in *The Taming of the Shrew* (II, i 397) Tranio somewhat obscurely says to the departing Gremio:

> A vengeance on your crafty wither'd hide!
> Yet I have faced it with a card of ten. . . .

he may or may not be referring to some forerunner of the game of brag or poker in which a ten is more valuable than a court card. But other references are figurative or unspecific, like – in *King John* (v, ii, 105) – the Dauphin's phrase to Pandulph, the papal legate:

> Have I not here the best cards for the game,
> To win this easy match play'd for a crown? . . .

or like Antony to Eros in *Antony and Cleopatra* concerning the Queen who has been reported dead (IV, xiv, 15):

> I made these wars for Egypt; and the Queen,—
> Whose heart I thought I had, for she had mine;
> Which, whilst it was mine, had annext unto't
> A million moe, now lost,—she, Eros, has

[39]

> Pack'd cards with Caesar, and false-play'd my glory
> Unto an enemy's triumph.—
> Nay, weep not, gentle Eros; there is left us
> Ourselves to end ourselves.

Shakespeare has, on the other hand, some few references to games that have vanished utterly. There was, for example, 'cherry pit' inadequately described as a children's game in which cherry-stones were thrown into a pit. This is mentioned in *Twelfth Night* (III, iv, 116) where Sir Toby says to Malvolio, who is being treated like a lunatic: 'Ay, Biddy, come with me. What, man! 'tis not for gravity to play at **cherry-pit** with Satan: ...' But it is not one of Sir Toby's more lucid observations.

Neither is Titania really lucid about the exact nature of the lost game or sport called 'nine-men's-morris' in *A Midsummer Night's Dream* (II, i, 94). When one first read it in the schoolroom in one's earliest teens, this long speech to Oberon, beginning 'These are the forgeries of jealousy', had all the magic of fairy-tale in its description of a mixed-up season:

> ... the green corn
> Hath rotted ere his youth attain'd a beard:
> The fold stands empty in the drownéd field,
> And crows are fatted with the murrion flock;
> The **nine-men's morris** is fill'd up with mud;
> And the quaint mazes in the wanton green,
> For lack of tread, are undistinguishable: ...

It would all seem to be a reference to the peculiarly nasty summer of the year 1594, which another Elizabethan poet, Charles Churchyard, specifically described:

> A colder time, in world was neuer seene
> The skies do lowre, the sun and moone waxe dim
> Sommer scarce knowne, but that the leues are greene
> The winter's waste, driues water ore the brim. ...

[40]

But Titania does it even better near the end of her same
speech (lines 111–14):

> ... the spring, the summer,
> The childing [= fruitful] autumn, angry winter, change
> Their wonted liveries; and the mazèd world,
> By their increase, now knows not which is which.

Fifty years ago one fondly imagined that Titania in the
beginning was referring to nine morris-dancers who exerted
themselves in quaint mazes. But many a subsequent scholar
has come along to assure us that the two items have no
connection – that 'nine-men's-morris' was a plot of green
turf cut into a sort of chessboard for youthful exercises, and
that 'quaint mazes' were reserved for youthful play as
distinct from youthful exercise. But the definition is too vague
to be very satisfying.

Chess itself, incidentally, seems to have no mention what-
soever, though it is one of the most ancient of games. The
stage-direction in the last act of *The Tempest* has a mention
of chess being played by Ferdinand and Miranda. This raises
a very interesting point. *The Tempest* did not reach publication
until the First Folio, seven years after Shakespeare's death,
and it is a generally accepted fact that the stage-directions,
which are unusually detailed, were not Shakespeare's own.
They also show remarkable variation. In some editions this
particular stage-direction runs:

> *Here Prospero discovers Ferdinand and Miranda,*
> *playing at chess.*

But in another there is a by no means unimportant difference:

> *The entrance of the Cell opens, and discovers*
> *Ferdinand and Miranda playing at chess.*

Clearly these are notes made by two quite distinct producers
for different productions of the play. Then again – if the

query can be made at this time of day – was it a game of chess or a card game? Note the dialogue of the players carefully (v, i, 172):

MIRANDA: Sweet lord, you play me false.
FERDINAND: No, my dear'st love,
  I would not for the world.
MIRANDA: Yes, for a score of kingdoms you should wrangle,
  And I would call it fair play.

Whatever Prospero's daughter may mean by her second statement, she clearly means by her first that her opponent is cheating. And the point is, whether one can cheat or 'play false' at chess where the pieces are seen by both players.

Lucio in *Measure for Measure* (I, ii, 180) at the end of a conversation with Claudio on the latter's doubtful future has a recondite reference to tick-tack which was an earlier form of backgammon. He regrets that his friend's life should be 'foolishly lost at a game of **tick-tack**'.

A single reference to 'football' is hardly complimentary. It is in the passage-at-arms between Kent and the impudent steward, Oswald, in *King Lear* (I, iv, 82):

OSWALD: I'll not be struck, my lord.
KENT: Nor tripped neither, you base *football* player.
                              (*Trips him up.*)

HUNTING AND COURSING

Hunting was, of course, mankind's chief occupation and preoccupation (in times of peace particularly), and Dr Spurgeon, who could hunt images as intensively as the Elizabethans could hunt deer or other game, finds no fewer than thirteen figures of speech deriving directly from the sport.

She also dares to jump to a personal conclusion about the poet himself (though with the wariness of the born scholar): 'From his hunting images generally, we gather that he clearly had often seen a deer hunt, and had enjoyed the clamorous echo of hounds and horn, but that although he knew all about driving the deer into nets ("into a toil"), and shooting them with a crossbow, he had probably not much experience of hunting deer with hounds only. He had certainly seen the stag at bay, surrounded by the yelping dogs, stained with the blood of their prey, but he himself shows little enthusiasm for the sport ... by far the larger number of what may be grouped under his hunting and woodcraft similes are concerned with the habits and behaviour of the deer and the eager skill of the questing hounds, rather than with the actual chase.'

She is no less revealing, and no less cautious, on the subject of the pursuit of the hare: 'I should imagine from his images that he knew personally much more about the Cotswold sport of coursing and of hunting the hare generally than he did of deer hunting.' She then refers to an astonishing passage in *Venus and Adonis* without actually quoting (lines 673–708) – of the hunted hare doubling and crossing to put the hounds off his scent; 'but here again', says Dr Spurgeon, 'it is noticeable that the intensity of his feeling is for the victim, rather than for the fun of the chase'. The speaker is Venus in the course of one of her lengthy exhortations to Adonis to refrain from the chase of the boar, or of anything else but her sweet self alone:

> But if thou needs wilt **hunt**, be ruled by me;
> Uncouple at the timorous flying hare,
> Or at the fox which lives by subtlety,
> Or at the roe which no encounter dare:

Pursue these fearful creatures o'er the downs,
And on thy well-breathed horse keep with thy hounds.

And when thou hast on foot the purblind hare,
Mark the poor wretch, to overshoot his troubles
How he outruns the wind, and with what care
He cranks and crosses with a thousand doubles:
    The many musets [= hedge-gaps] through the which he goes
    Are like a labyrinth to amaze his foes.

Sometimes he runs among a flock of sheep,
To make the cunning hounds mistake their smell,
And sometimes where earth-delving conies keep,
To stop the loud pursuers in their yell;
    And sometimes sorteth with a herd of deer:
    Danger deviseth shifts, wit waits on fear:

For there his smell with others being mingled,
The hot scent-snuffing hounds are driven to doubt,
Ceasing their clamorous cry till they have singled
With much ado the cold fault cleanly out;
    Then do they spend their mouths: Echo replies,
    As if another chase were in the skies.

By this, poor Wat, far off upon a hill,
Stands on his hinder legs with list'ning ear,
To hearken if his foes pursue him still: . . .

Yes, one would agree that the phrase 'poor Wat' for the poor hare is far more likely to be the voice of the poet than that of the yearning goddess.

See also BOAR-HUNTING.

LOVING AND LUSTING

Here, of course, the scope is infinite, just as the subject is inexhaustible. But by way of distraction or as a diversion for flagging readers one might offer here a questionnaire out of nine or ten plays in all.

Who then, made the following utterances, declarations, or avowals, and in what play? Each of them directly concerns the subject of love or mutual devotion.

1

I am no pilot; yet, wert thou as far
As that vast shore wash'd with the furthest sea,
I would adventure for such merchandise.

2

But trust me, gentleman, I'll prove more true
Than those that have more cunning to be strange.
I should have been more strange, I must confess,
But that thou overheard'st, ere I was ware,
My true love's passion: therefore pardon me;
And not impute this yielding to light love, . . .

3

What is't? a spirit?
Lord, how it looks about! Believe me, sir,
It carries a brave form:—but 'tis a spirit.
. . . I might call him
A thing divine; for nothing natural
I ever saw so noble.

4

I do love nothing in the world so well as you:
is not that strange?

[45]

5

How all the other passions fleet to air,—
As doubtful thoughts, and rash-embraced despair,
And shuddering fear, and green-eyed jealousy!
O love, be moderate; allay thy ecstasy;
In measure rain thy joy; scant this excess!
I feel too much thy blessing: make it less,
For fear I surfeit!

6

You are my true and honourable wife;
As dear to me as are the ruddy drops
That visit my sad heart.

7

I durst, my lord, to wager she is honest,
Lay down my soul at stake: if you think other,
Remove your thought,—it doth abuse your bosom.
If any wretch have put this in your head,
Let heaven requite it with the serpent's curse!
For, if she be not honest, chaste, and true,
There's no man happy; the purest of their wives
Is foul as slander.

8

What win I, if I gain the thing I seek?
A dream, a breath, a froth of fleeting joy.
Who buys a minute's worth to wail a week?
Or sells eternity to get a toy?
For one sweet grape who will the vine destroy?
 Or what fond beggar, but to touch the crown,
 Would with the sceptre straight be strucken down?

9

If it be love indeed, tell me how much.
There's beggary in the love that can be reckon'd.

I'll set a bourn how far to be beloved.
Then must thou needs find out new heaven, new earth.

1. It is Romeo making the least conventional and most
   imaginative of all his compliments to Juliet in the balcony
   scene (II, i, 124–6).

2. It is Juliet to Romeo (II, i, 142–7), twice using the stressed
   word 'strange' in its sense of 'distant' or 'reserved'. (The
   slightly unexpected 'gentleman' – though, of course, it
   occurs in the text – is a deliberate 'red herring' for the
   solver.)

3. It is Miranda's utterance when she first sets eyes on
   Ferdinand in *The Tempest* (I, ii, 410–20).

4. It is Bendick at last bursting into flame with Beatrice after
   three whole acts of sparks and smoke – *Much Ado About
   Nothing* (IV, i, 266).

5. It is Portia speaking to herself (though the passage is not
   marked as a soliloquy or an aside) while Bassanio is in
   process of choosing the right casket in *The Merchant of
   Venice* (III, ii, 108–14).

6. It is Brutus addressing the other Portia, Cato's daughter,
   in what may be called a spasm of wedded ecstasy – *Julius
   Caesar* (II, i, 288–90).

7. It is Emilia addressing Othello (IV, ii, 12–19) – with
   admirable frankness; though, as always, we note that with
   just a shade more of such frankness she might have obviated
   the whole tragedy.

8. It is Tarquin expressing a qualm at the pleasure, intense
   but brief, he may derive from the execution of his fell
   purpose. (From a poem not a play, it is true – *The Rape of
   Lucrece*, 211–17. But Tarquin's moment of compunction
   is almost as dramatic as anything in the tragedies.)

9. & 10. Both are snatches of dialogue – the opening dialogue
   – between Cleopatra and Antony, and in that order – in

Antony and Cleopatra (I, i, 14–17). Let the interchange be repeated here for absolute clarity's sake:

CLEOPATRA: If it be love indeed, tell me how much.
ANTONY: There's beggary in the love that can be reckon'd.
CLEOPATRA: I'll set a bourn how far to be belov'd.
ANTONY: Then must thou needs find out new heaven, new earth.

There is the whole essence of the play in this double interchange, and the four lines have very seldom, in our experience, been given anything like their just deliberation. For in these four lines Antony and Cleopatra reveal to us that they are boundlessly and limitlessly in love for the rest of eternity.

These four lines do not absolutely open the great play, though they very nearly do so. In a manner that is utterly without precedent this interchange is preceded by a speech of thirteen lines uttered by a minor character called Philo to another minor character called Demetrius who has not a word to say in return. In the theatre, this opening speech is almost always handed to some minor actor who almost invariably fails to realize that he can here, if he knows how, set the whole mood of the play. It behoves this actor to give the tragedy its whole point, its *donnée*, in a matter of something around one hundred words, the very first of which is the negative particle which anyone – who had not *Antony and Cleopatra* in mind – would deny could possibly set off any play of any sort on its course. It is the particle 'Nay', and this is how it is breathtakingly done and proceeded with:

> Nay, but this dotage of our general's
> O'erflows the measure: those his goodly eyes,
> That o'er the files and musters of the war
> Have glow'd like plated Mars, now bend, now turn,
> The office and devotion of their view
> Upon a tawny front: his captain's heart,
> Which in the scuffles of great fights hath burst

> The buckles on his breast, reneges all temper,
> And is become the bellows and the fan
> To cool a gipsy's lust. Look where they come:
> Take but good note, and you shall see in him
> The triple pillar of the world transform'd
> Into a strumpet's fool: behold and see.

This prelude spoken, there is an annunciatory trumpet and then there enters our mighty duo with eternity already in their lips and eyes.

Only once, in the twelve revivals of this rarely-revived play that one has had to the luck to behold in a matter of twenty-five years – only once was Philo's prelude properly and more than adequately delivered. 'Nay' itself was loaded with protestation and resentment. The words 'tawny' and 'gipsy' and 'strumpet' were each given a sharp emphasis to reveal the common soldier's scorn at his general's thraldom. Almost all of the rest of the speech burned with pride at the valour of the great Triumvir – 'the triple pillar of the world' – and, at one and the same time, burned with indignation at the Queen who was manifestly reducing him to servitude and folly and eventual cowardice and shame.

This occasion was in an anonymous revival of the play by the Marlowe Society at Cambridge away back in the spring of 1946. It was Ivor Brown, of all good judges, who strongly recommended the present writer to cancel any other engagement for that week's end and see this play-production on the Saturday. One did, and the experience was unforgettable.

The direction was by George Rylands, the presiding genius of the Marlowe Society. It was in our experience the best of all his Shakespearean productions. Here was a director who seemed always far more at home with amateurs than with professionals. Untrained and malleable material always did bring out the best in him. He had a particular gift for ensuring that Shakespeare spoke for himself through his students. It is only another way of saying that he insisted on every word being clearly heard and with its proper emphasis down to the smallest syllable of the smallest word in the smallest part.

In this great particular play characters like Agrippa, the Soothsayer, Scarus and even Pompey are usually so subordinated by the almost over-rich substance of the writing as to go almost unnoticed. But all such characters were on this occasion at Cambridge clearly individualized. One had never heard Enobarbus' line: 'He will to his Egyptian dish again!' better or more scathingly pointed. 'O, rare for Antony!' – as Agrippa exclaims. But the whole thing was revelationary from the very start – from Philo's thirteen lines of prelude. (Philo has an unremarkable three or four lines at the end of the scene, and nothing else at all to say in the whole play, such was Shakespeare's largesse when writing in the high Roman fashion.)

For Cleopatra herself George Rylands happily discovered a young woman, neither professional nor in the least beautiful to watch or gaze upon, who had that attribute to which the Shakespearean scholar in him attached a far greater importance – a warm, variable, and expressive voice which she had enough art to use intelligently and obediently. Between them the player and her director conveyed an astonishing amount of that Eternal Womanliness – that *mélange* of vanity, allurement, spite, adorableness, cruelty, tenderness, witchery, ardour, guile, and won't-take-No-for-an-answer-hood – which has been the despair of many of our very best professional actresses.

It is a significant fact that the best English actresses of the last two centuries have not even attempted the formidable part of Shakespeare's Cleopatra – not Siddons nor Ellen Terry nor Mrs Campbell; just as among the supreme actors of the same period, neither Kean nor Kemble nor Henry

Irving nor Forbes-Robertson ever attempted her counterpart Antony. It is true that Kemble wanted to revive the play with himself as Antony and his sister, the great Mrs Siddons, as Cleopatra. The latter would not risk failing in the part and refrained from even trying with her brother or anyone else. She gave the superb reason that she thought the representation might be too much for her public. And it is on record that when she declined the part of Cleopatra she said to Kemble that 'she should hate herself if she should play the part as it ought to be played'.

In consequence of its being neglected, or at least resisted, by all our supreme acting couples in the last 150 years, this great play has inspired no major dramatic criticism between Hazlitt and Ivor Brown himself. Hazlitt, who saw only Charles Mayne Young and Helen Faucit as the mighty duo in 1813, was nevertheless a great dramatic critic and could write of the play in his study as though he had seen it greatly done in the mind's eye; he concludes his general essay on the play itself: 'Shakespeare's genius has spread over the whole play a richness like the overflowing of the Nile.'

This is an example of the grand manner; and Ivor Brown himself attains to the same over and over again when he comes to deal with this, his first favourite among all the plays, in his *magnum opus*, the book simply and sufficiently entitled *Shakespeare*. This work first appeared in the year 1949, the fruit of a lifetime of study, and it should be made compulsive study – indeed, it probably is so – in all schools and theatres where Shakespeare is loved and read and acted.

*   *   *

Mr Ivor Brown in the middle of his great book – no less a judge than Bernard Shaw described it quite categorically as 'the best book about Shakespeare yet written' – has two consecutive chapters entitled 'Woman Colour'd Ill' and 'Lass

Unparallel'd'. These are the heart of his study, and the heart-beat is almost audible as one reads.

The chapters form a closely-sustained argument to the effect that the mysterious Dark Lady was as important in Shakespeare's life as the character of Cleopatra was pre-eminent in his life-work. The scholar-critic thinks – and makes us think with him – that the Dark Lady (whosoever she was) dominated and devastated Shakespeare far more profoundly than did his wife, his best friend, or his troops of friends. The scholar-critic similarly thinks – and makes us think with him – that Cleopatra is by far the most complex character who ever beguiled his brain and challenged his creative powers to limn her satisfactorily and consistently.

He is careful not to identify these two great influences, one of them upon Shakespeare's life, and the other upon Shakespeare's life-work. But then comes a paragraph when he has just mentioned the death or vanishing from his life of the Dark Lady, and when the two seem almost to merge and become one:

She was dead: or she had moved altogether away from the humble sphere of a player-poet. That would have meant that she had left London, for the English capital of Shakespeare's day – no longer than Oxford in our time – was no easy place in which to miss or to avoid people of note or notoriety. Had she moved onwards and upwards in her conquering progress the player-poet would hardly have forgiven her: and *Antony and Cleopatra* is essentially a hymn of forgiveness. By the time that Shakespeare had finished with the Dark Lady in this tremendous tragedy, she had declared her immortal longings and made Death proud to take her. Almost one might say that the 'daughter of the game' was now a royal spirit, soaring, on the wings of her own beauty, into an empyrean; the whitely wanton, and at other times gipsy wanton, had, through sheer integrity of wantonness and complete concentration upon passion, somehow become in tune with the infinite.

He continues no less superbly:

The last two acts of *Antony and Cleopatra*, acts which contain the most heart-searching poetry that Shakespeare ever wrote, cannot be interpreted in any other way than as a salute to love which tolerates no mitigation, to a lavishness and a luxury which count the world well lost if love be satisfied. They are also a farewell. The Dark Lady may or may not have been dead. But something snapped. The ecstasy and the agony were over.

Elsewhere, within the same two chapters, Mr Brown divagates with the serene impartiality of Goethe himself:

His [Antony's] first speech of any length is a disclaimer of political ambition, since the summit of life is to be discovered in the map of love and not in any chart of earthly kingdoms.

> Let Rome in Tiber melt, and the wide arch
> Of the ranged empire fall! Here is my space.
> Kingdoms are clay: our dungy earth alike
> Feeds beast as man: the nobleness of life
> Is to do thus: when such a mutual pair,
> And such a twain can do't, in which I bind,
> On pain of punishment, the world to weet
> We stand up peerless.

'The nobleness of life'. To that ideal of love-over-all Antony is true: he tosses away his universe for a woman: and the very size of that sacrifice, the strength of the decision, seem to fire Shakespeare's keenest admiration. It is impossible to read or see this play without conviction as to where the playwright's sympathy is placed. He no longer rails at the tyranny of passion; he accepts it, even reveres it, so it be tyrannical enough. It has been well said that gambling is only contemptible if carried on within your means. For Shakespeare, in the mood of this play, this view holds of wenching as well as of wagering. Sexual surrender can lose its shabbiness by loyalty to its own excess.

Time and again Shakespeare, in Sonnet and in play, had cried out against this excess, the expense of spirit in a waste of shame [Sonnet

129]. But now he has lost that careful temper: the lurking Puritan within him has been ousted for a season by the forthright hedonist. So the play moves through its early and not easily staged acts with their abundance of classical history, vexatious to a modern audience, and their manifold changes of scene, as it were a film unfolding. For these reasons and because it needs almost superhuman perform-ance and is lost without the best in casts and direction, *Antony and Cleopatra* will rarely, if ever, be 'good box-office'. The action scrambles forward until it reaches the peaks of the last two acts, peaks not only of the play's own composition but of the Shake-spearean workmanship which gives to every word a higher power. It is in the closing passages of this tragedy that we come, in my opinion, closer to Shakespeare's heart than anywhere else, even in *Hamlet*. The temper and opinion there revealed are certainly not characteristic: Shakespeare was, on the whole, a temperate man, careful of his money, nervous that his sensibility might betray him, afraid of his passions. But upon this occasion, he stripped moderation from his mind and paid salutation to a man who would keep nothing.

> His legs bestrid the ocean: his rear'd arm
> Crested the world; his voice was propertied
> As all the tunèd spheres, and that to friends;
> But when he meant to quail and shake the orb,
> He was as rattling thunder. For his bounty,
> There was no winter in't; an autumn 'twas
> That grew the more by reaping: his delights
> Were dolphin-like; they show'd his back above
> The element they lived in: in his livery
> Walked crowns and crownets; realms and islands were
> As plates dropt from his pocket.

He paid salutation no less to the woman who would take all. Half-measures, prudent courses, on the part of either of them would have lost their creator's enraptured obeisance. To find nobleness in such squanderings of property and power was not his enduring philosophy; far from it. But when the vision of such bounty did blaze upon his eyes, he wrote with an intensity, even with a sublimity, not elsewhere equalled in the canon. Cleopatra has the phrase 'less unparallel'd' dropped upon her dying body: it is this concept of supremacy, of uniqueness ('we stand up peerless') and of absolute dedication to love which upon this occasion evoked from him those breath-taking achievements, the death-scenes of Antony and Cleopatra: self-slaughtered both, they die in the high Roman way and make death their proud partners on the last of all the Orient's soft beds.

Mr Ivor Brown continues in this 'high Roman fashion' anent the great play's ending:

For my part, I read the great finale of *Antony and Cleopatra* as a valediction. Something had ended in Shakespeare's life. His health was better, his grip upon himself far more assured than when he was pouring out – one might almost say retching up – the lazar-house cursings of *Timon*. My submission is that because the Dark Lady would neither entrance nor madden him again, he could look back and withhold the stinging phrase with which he had encouraged the ebon hair and eyes, the white and blue-veined skin of that exquisite but 'jigging' wantonness. He would do more than spare, since now, being released, he was free to praise and, because she would not hurt him again, he would forgive, he would adore. For certainly both Antony and Cleopatra died enobled and esteemed. The world first bidden to 'weet' that they stand up peerless sees them lie down no less supreme in their own reckless, lavish, superbly improvident kind,

> Now boast thee, death, in thy possession lies
> A lass unparallel'd.

The brief, affectionate 'lass', the weighty rolling 'unparallel'd' – they are typical Shakespearean magic. They are also a proclamation of pardon, a statement of forgiveness as well as of farewell – to the wanton Cleopatra certainly, and, as I think, to another also, the poet's own love of ecstasy and despair. This, at least, is beyond dispute: that if we owe some of the Sonnets and all of *Antony and Cleopatra* to a Lady Anon, Tudor-Jacobean beauty of her day, then our debt to the unnamed, elusive creature outranges calculation.

MUSIC, HO!

The best-known things about music are too familiar, but they cannot be ignored. Things like Lorenzo's lines to young Jessica in the moonlit garden of Belmont in *The Merchant of Venice* (v, i, 83).

> The man that hath no **music** in himself,
> Nor is not moved with concord of sweet sounds,
> Is fit for treasons, stratagems, and spoils;
> The motions of his spirit are dull as night,
> And his affections dark as Erebus:
> Let no such man be trusted.—Mark the **music.**

(It could readily be argued that this is not strictly true, though it is divinely phrased.)

We like the three last words particularly since they imply that Lorenzo has run out of platitudes on the subject.

We may also note that in the theatre the part of Lorenzo, usually given to some young actor unable to disguise his liking for the sound of his own voice, has been docked by the director of some much better lines in the same long speech (v, i, 70), uttered when Jessica has said that music makes her melancholy:

> The reason is, your spirits are attentive:
> For do but note a wild and wanton herd,
> Or race of youthful and unhandled colts,
> Fetching mad bounds, bellowing, and neighing loud,
> Which is the hot condition of their blood;
> If they but hear perchance a trumpet sound,
> Or any air of **music** touch their ears,
> You shall perceive them make a mutual stand,
> Their savage eyes turn'd to a modest gaze,
> By the sweet power of **music**: . . .

[56]

Still better known is the opening of *Twelfth Night* (i, i, 1) where the love-sick Orsino demands a dose of music as though it were a dose of medicine, however exquisite his phrases:

> If **music** be the food of love, play on;
> Give me excess of it, that, surfeiting,
> The appetite may sicken, and so die.—
> That strain again!—it had a dying fall:
> O, it came o'er my ear like the sweet sough,
> That breathes upon a bank of violets,
> Stealing and giving odour!—Enough; no more;
> 'Tis not so sweet now as it was before.

Parenthetically let it be noted that we use the New Cambridge edition's 'sough' instead of 'sound' or 'south' (which was Pope's suggestion). 'Sough' was the expressive word used by William Hazlitt for the tender voice used by Edmund Kean's Othello towards his Desdemona, 'like the soughing of the wind through cedars'.

It is Othello himself, by the way, who reminds us that Shakespeare can say as much, on a subject like music, in an aside of a single line as in a set piece of many lines. In the throes of Othello's jealous rage at Desdemona (and at the height of Iago's evil provocation) he has this of his wife's singing (iv, i, 189): '. . . an admirable **musician**! O, she will sing the savageness out of a bear! . . .'

Almost with his last breath old John of Gaunt in *King Richard II* (ii, i, 12) has a beautiful line that deserves isolation: 'The setting sun, and **music** at the close.'

Cleopatra, with her Antony absent in Rome, begins a scene (*Antony and Cleopatra*, ii, v, 1) with a demand for the solace of sound: 'Give me some **music**,—**music**, moody food Of us that trade in love' (whereupon an Attendant crying: 'The **music**, ho!' provided the late Constant Lambert with the title for his capital book of musical criticism).

Pericles falls asleep in the arms of his restored daughter Marina, in *Pericles, Prince of Tyre* (v, i, 232):

> ... I hear
> Most heavenly **music**!
> It nips me unto listening, and thick slumber
> Hangs upon mine eyes: let me rest.

And even in that inconsiderable play, *The Two Gentlemen of Verona*, Proteus makes preparation for his serenade to Silvia in language of a lovely simplicity (iv, ii, 16):

> But here comes Thurio: now must we to her window,
> And give some evening **music** to her ear.

Other references to music are, of course, beyond number, and we can cite only a few. But in *Antony and Cleopatra* itself we must not overlook – as the play's directors so often do in the theatre – this magical little scene. It is but thirty lines in all; it happens on the ramparts of Cleopatra's palace at Alexandria; and music is an integral part of it (iv, iii, 1):

Enter two Soldiers to their guard

1.S. Brother, good night: to-morrow is the day.
2.S. It will determine one way: fare you well.
    Heard you of nothing strange about the streets?
1.S. Nothing. What news?
2.S. Belike 'tis but a rumour. Good night to you.
1.S. Well, sir, good night.

Enter other Soldiers

2.S. Soldiers, have careful watch.
3.S. And you. Good night, good night.

They place themselves in every corner of the stage

4.S. Here we: and if to-morrow
    Our navy thrive, I have an absolute hope
    Our landmen will stand up.

3.S.	'Tis a brave army,
	And full of purpose.
	Music of the hautboys as under the stage
4.S.	Peace! what noise?
1.S.	List, list!
2.S.	Hark!
1.S.	**Music** i'the air.
3.S.	Under the earth.
4.S.	It signs [= bodes] well, does it not?
3.S.	No.
1.S.	Peace, I say!
	What should this mean?
2.S.	'Tis the god Hercules, whom Antony loved,
	Now leaves him.
1.S.	Walk; let's see if other watchmen
	Do hear what we do?
2.S.	How now, masters!
All	(*speaking together*) How now!
	How now! Do you hear this?
1.S.	Ay; is't not strange?
3.S.	Do you hear, masters? do you hear?
1.S.	Follow the noise so far as we have quarter;
	Let's see how it will give off.
All.	Content. 'Tis strange.

The opportunities here for a musical composer of genius are immense, and they do not seem – in our time at least – to have been grasped. The dramatic intensity of the little scene is also very remarkable (and would seem to have been insufficiently remarked – even by Granville-Barker who at least commends the notable economy of the dialogue). The line about Hercules is sheer inspiration, and those who meekly assume that the whole thing derives from Plutarch may like to read the corresponding Plutarch passage and to note that Hercules gets no particular mention, also that instead of this magical and mystical surmise there is a long image of a corybantic

[59]

procession which Shakespeare wisely disregarded as an irrelevant episode:

Furthermore, the self same night within little of midnight, when all the city was quiet, full of fear and sorrow, thinking what would be the issue and end of this war, it is said that suddenly they heard a marvellous sweet harmony of sundry sorts of instruments of music, with the cry of a multitude of people, as they had been dancing and had sung as they used in Bacchus' feasts, with movings and turnings after the manner of the Satyrs. And it seemed that this dance went through the city unto the gate that opened to the enemies, and that all the troupe who made the noise they heard went out of the city at that gate. Now such as in reason sought the depth of the interpretation of this wonder, thought that it was the god to whom Antonius bore singular devotion to counterfeit and resemble him, that did forsake them.

No mention, be it noted, of Shakespeare's six sentries, or of their inarticulate speech, or of the subterranean *source* of the music they suddenly hear, or of its being played by hautboys, nor any mention of the god Hercules by name.

It is not contested that Shakespeare could take his good where he found it, or knew where it was to be found; and how much of it to take, and how little, for his own poetic purpose.

MUSIC-MAKING

There are so many ways of music-making that it seems best to arrange the instruments in alphabetical order.

See also under SONGS AND SINGING.

BAGPIPES. Salarino in *The Merchant of Venice* has a picturesque phrase about men who are easily amused and 'laugh, like parrots, at a **bag-piper**' (I, i, 53). Shylock in the same play talks of some other men who, 'when the **bag-pipe** sings i'th' nose, Cannot contain their urine' (IV, i, 49). And a few lines later this same Jew refers to the same instrument, semi-contemptuously, as a 'woollen **bag-pipe**'.

At the Sheep Fair in *The Winter's Tale* a Servant tells the Clown of the arrival of Autolycus (IV, iii, 181): 'O master, if you did but hear the pedlar at the door, you would never dance again after a tabor and pipe; no, the **bagpipe** could not move you; he sings several tunes faster than you'll tell money; he utters them as he had eaten ballads, and all men's ears grew to his tunes.'

Falstaff describes himself to Prince Hal as being as melancholy as 'the drone of a Lincolnshire **bagpipe**' in *King Henry IV, Part One* (I, ii, 75).

These are Shakespeare's only mentions of this instrument (of both torture and delight). It exists nowhere in *Macbeth*. It is not (in truth and *pace* Scotland) a particularly Scottish instrument. One has heard it played in Lombardy and northern Greece and (or something very like it) even in the heart of Turkey.

★   ★   ★

CYMBALS. In the build-up for the very last entrance of Coriolanus, a mere Second Messenger (V, iv, 50) has a finely sonorous little speech containing Shakespeare's only mention of the cymbals:

> Why, hark you!
> The trumpets, sackbuts, psaltries, and fifes,
> Tabors, and **cymbals**, and the shouting Romans,
> Make the sun dance. Hark you!

★   ★   ★

DRUMS. There are drums innumerable, and one must be eclectic. Another splendid line for an important character's entrance is the Third Witch's 'A **drum**, a **drum**! Macbeth doth come.' (*Macbeth*, I, iii, 30). (And see under TRUMPETS.)

Philip of France is warned by his ambassador Chatillon of

the approach of the English king and his wife, niece, and retinue – in *King John* (II, i, 76):

> CHATILLON: The interruption of their churlish **drums**
>   Cuts off more circumstances: they are at hand,
>   To parley or to fight; therefore prepare.
> KING PHILIP: How much unlook'd for is this expedition!

A warm French welcome!

Alternately purring like a peaceful tom-cat and roaring like a martial lion, Bolingbroke in *King Richard II* (III, iii, 40) returns from banishment in a mixed-up state, but speaking in splendid style:

> Provided that my banishment repeal'd
> And lands restor'd again be freely granted:
> If not, I'll use th' advantage of my power,
> And lay the summer's dust with showers of blood
> Rain'd from the wounds of slaughter'd Englishmen:
> The which, how far off from the mind of Bolingbroke
> It is, such crimson tempest should bedrench
> The fresh green lap of fair King Richard's land,
> My stooping duty tenderly shall show.
> Go, signify as much, while here we march
> Upon the grassy carpet of this plain.
> Let's march without the noise of threatening **drum**, ...

It is given to a Third Senator to announce Alcibiades and his 'terrible approach' in *Timon of Athens* (V, ii, 15):

> The enemies' **drum** is heard, and fearful scouring
> Doth choke the air with dust: in, and prepare:
> Ours is the fall, I fear; our foes the snare.

And there is in *All's Well That Ends Well* some distinctly tiresome word-play on 'drum', and 'drums', and 'John Drum' (to whom Parolles is compared repeatedly in III, vi). If one is obliged to study this scene it may be helpful to know that Shakespeare's contemporary, John Marston, wrote a play called *Jack Drum's Entertainment* which is reputed to be a satire on Ben Jonson; also that to this day 'drummed out' is military slang for a soldier ejected from his regiment for insubordination (or from a party for drunkenness).

✱   ✱   ✱

FIFES (See under CYMBALS).

FLUTES. These are played in Shakespeare only in *Antony and Cleopatra,* and on two different occasions. One is in Enobarbus' justly celebrated description of the royal barge (II, ii, 198):

> . . . the oars were silver,
> Which to the tune of **flutes** kept stroke, and made
> The water which they beat to follow faster,
> As amorous of their strokes. . . .

The other is at the end of quite a party in Pompey's galley when only Enobarbus and Menas are left aboard. And if Enobarbus is not, so to speak, half-seas-over and Menas the other half-seas-over then their author cannot communicate the fact in likely dialogue (II, vii, 130):

ENOBARBUS (*to the departing Pompey*): Take heed you fall not.
    Menas, I'll not on shore.
MENAS: No, to my cabin.—
    These drums!—these trumpets, **flutes**! what!
    Let Neptune hear we bid a loud farewell
    To these great fellows: sound and be hang'd, and sound out!
               [*a flourish with drums*
ENOBARBUS: Hoo! says a'.—There's my cap.
MENAS: Hoo!—Noble captain, come. [*exeunt*

'Hoo!' is a notable interjection occurring nowhere else in the works of Shakespeare. One must take it to be something between a scream and a roar.

✱   ✱   ✱

HARPS. These are few and far between, but always interestingly and sometimes surprisingly introduced.

First a clash of temper and taste between the hot English Hotspur and the blunt Welsh Glendower in *King Henry IV, Part One* (III, i, 115):

HOTSPUR: I'll have it so: a little charge will do it.
GLENDOWER: I'll not have it alter'd.
HOTSPUR: Will not you?
GLENDOWER: No, nor you shall not.
HOTSPUR: Who shall say me nay?
GLENDOWER: Why, that will I.
HOTSPUR: Let me not understand you, then; speak it in Welsh.
GLENDOWER: I can speak English, lord, as well as you;
   For I was train'd up in the English court;
   Where, being but young, I framèd to the **harp**
   Many an English ditty lovely well,
   And gave the tongue a helpful ornament,—
   A virtue that was never seen in you.
HOTSPUR: Marry, And I am glad of it with all my heart:
   I had rather be a kitten, and cry mew,
   Than one of these same metre ballet-mongers; . . .

Next, Mowbray of Norfolk to his king, who has just banished him to live abroad for ever – *King Richard II* (I, iii, 159):

   The language I have learn'd these forty years,
   My native English, now I must forgo:
   And now my tongue's use is to me no more
   Than an unstringed viol or a **harp**;
   Or like a cunning instrument cased up,
   Or, being open, put into his hands
   That knows no touch to tune the harmony: . . .

Then, a piece of blazing obscurity in *The Tempest* (II, i, 84) from that cipher of a character, Prospero's usurping brother, Antonio. In the very middle of a yawn-making argument between these shipwrecked nobleman and their retinue – an ineffably tedious and witless discussion as to whether or not Dido could be called the Widow Dido after Aeneas left her, and whether it was Tunis she inhabited or Carthage – then Antonio suddenly says of the elderly Gonzalo (who thought 'twas Carthage): 'His word is more than the miraculous **harp**.'

Scholar Henry Hudson here excels himself by telling us that this 'miraculous harp' or lyre belonged to Amphion, king of Thebes; that it was given to him by the god Mercury for his great love of music, and that the walls of Thebes miraculously rose up in answer to his playing. This scholar goes on to quote William Wordsworth: 'The gift to King Amphion, that wall'd a city with its melody', and finally surpasses himself by confuting the non-stop noblemen in their prattle: 'Tunis is in fact supposed to be on or near the site of ancient Carthage.'

Finally we may note with a chuckle Theseus' prompt response in *A Midsummer Night's Dream* (v, i, 44) when offered as part of his wedding-entertainment something called 'The battle with the Centaurs, to be sung By an Athenian eunuch to the **harp**'. Theseus said: 'We'll none of that.'

*   *   *

HAUTBOYS. The word is an earlier form of 'oboe', and it occurs only in a long and capital speech of Falstaff at the end of Act III of *King Henry IV, Part Two*. He is describing the almost repellent leanness of Justice Shallow, young or old. Shallow appears to have been what Ayrshire children of my young days would call a 'skinnymalink'; and Sir John gobbles him up in soliloquy (III, ii, 336):

'. . . for you might have thrust him and all his apparel into an eel-skin; the case of a treble **hautboy** was a mansion for him, a court:—and now has he land and beefs. Well, I'll be acquainted with him, if I return; . . . if the young dace be a bait for the old pike, I see no reason, in the law of nature, but I may snap at him. Let time shape, and there an end.'

But hautboys are mentioned also in a stage-direction as providing subterranean music in a most strange little scene in *Antony and Cleopatra* (see under MUSIC HO !).

★　　★　　★

LUTES. The simple beauty of this little word 'lute' – it signifies an obsolete form of harp with a kind of fiddleback to it – inspires many a lovely line here and there throughout the plays.

'For Orpheus' **lute** was strung with poets' sinews', says Proteus in *Two Gentlemen of Verona* (III, ii, 78).

'As bright Apollo's **lute**, strung with his hair', says Berowne in *Love's Labour's Lost* (IV, iii, 340).

'To the lascivious pleasing of a **lute**', says Gloster in *King Richard III* (I, i, 13).

'Take thy **lute**, wench: my soul grows sad with troubles', says Queen Katharine in *King Henry VIII* (III, i, 1), and the Wench immediately complies with the ravishing song that begins:

> Orpheus with his **lute** made trees,
> And the mountain-tops that freeze,
> > Bow themselves, when he did sing:
> To his music plants and flowers
> Ever sprung; as sun and showers
> > There had made a lasting spring.

And old Gower the Chorus, at the beginning of Act IV (Prologue, 25) of *Pericles, Prince of Tyre*, talks of the lost daughter Marina

> . . . when to the **lute**
> She sung, and made the night-bird mute,
> That still records with moan; . . .

Other Elizabethans preceded and followed Shakespeare with lute-song. The courtier and poet, Sir Thomas Wyatt, concluded a ditty of his with the line: 'My lute, be still, for I have done', and Wyatt died twelve years before Shakespeare was born. And Thomas Campion, poet and musician who sang his own songs to his own accompaniment, has one beginning: 'When to her lute Corinna sings'. Campion was to die in 1620, four years after Shakespeare's death.

*   *   *

ORGAN. The two references to the noblest of musical instruments are both figurative and indirect but also very fine.

One is in *The Tempest* where Alonso, King of Naples, has almost his only solemn speech (III, iii, 95), imagining the death of his son Ferdinand:

> O, it is monstrous, monstrous!
> Methought the billows spoke, and told me of it;
> The winds did sing it to me; and the thunder,
> That deep and dreadful **organ**-pipe, pronounced
> The name of Prosper: it did bass my trespass.
> Therefore my son i'the ooze is bedded; and
> I'll seek him deeper than e'er plummet sounded,
> And with him there lie mudded.

The other moving and solemn passage is spoken by Prince Henry in *King John* (V, vii, 20) just before the king, poisoned and dying, is borne into the orchard at Swinstead Abbey:

> 'Tis strange that death should sing.—
> I am the cygnet to this pale faint swan,
> Who chants a doleful hymn to his own death,
> And from the **organ**-pipe of frailty sings
> His soul and body to their lasting rest.

*   *   *

[67]

PIPES. The shepherd's pipe, usually accompanied by the tabor or the drum, provided peaceful music as distinct from the martial sort. Thus Benedick in *Much Ado About Nothing* (II, iii, 12) describes Claudio as having turned from being a soldier into a man of peace: 'I have known when there was no music with him but the drum and the fife; and now had he rather hear the tabor and the **pipe**.' The same two instruments are coupled again by the Servant in *The Winter's Tale* on the arrival of Autolycus the pedlar (see above under BAGPIPES).

Again it is pipes, of a sort unspecified, which provide in *Much Ado About Nothing* (V, iv, 128) the dance with which that comedy gaily concludes, with Benedick having the very last word: 'Strike up, **pipers**.' And 'shepherds **pipe** on oaten straws' in the Song of Spring near the end of *Love's Labour's Lost* (V, ii, 896).

*   *   *

PSALTERIES. The only mention of these ancient instruments – a kind of dulcimer but with strings plucked with a plectrum – is in *Coriolanus* (see above under CYMBALS).

*   *   *

REBECK. This ancient instrument again has only one mention, and that is not as an instrument but as the surname of a musician in *Romeo and Juliet*. He is one of the small band which presumably plays at old Capulet's party and certainly plays at Juliet's funeral ceremony. He is 'Hugh Rebeck', and his fellow players – or the only two who play or speak (IV, v, 96) – are 'Simon Catling' and 'James Soundpost'.

The rebeck was a three-stringed instrument played with a bow. A catling was a small-sized lute-string made of catgut. A soundpost – still very much in existence – is a peg between the back and the belly of any stringed instrument, used as an essential support.

These provide goodly names for musicians. It is, none the less, a system of nomenclature which Shakespeare does not greatly or regularly favour, though he did well with 'Mistress Overdone' for the brothel-keeper in *Measure for Measure* and with 'Doll Tearsheet' for the witty slut in *King Henry IV, Part Two*.

★   ★   ★

RECORDERS. 'Come, some music! come, the recorders!' (*Hamlet*, III, ii, 309). The speaker is, of course, Hamlet, and the 'Recorders Scene' is said to be one of the highlights of the distracted Prince's role. Is it, really and truly?

Hamlet calls for one or two of these instruments – a wooden whistle not unlike a tin-whistle – and there is some delay in the actors' bringing them. One perfectly understands the delay. The actors are presumed to have accompanied their little play, *The Murder of Gonzago*, with recorders and some other instrument; and may therefore be supposed to have had these instruments ready to hand. But why should the Players immediately oblige, or oblige at all?

They have been reasonably well welcomed on arrival. But they are hardly settled down for a night or two at the Danish Court before the Prince of Denmark has given them an exceptionally severe and critical lecture on the art of play-acting (see under ACTING), and they have also been asked to absorb a speech, which is part of the Prince's own purpose and which eventually ensures their little play having a reception which is not so much 'mixed' as disastrously broken off before its conclusion (whatever that conclusion may have been).

Admittedly the third act of *Hamlet* is the most dramatic single act in the whole of the literature of the theatre. But at least one of its fervid admirers questions the 'Recorders Scene'. Every Hamlet in one's own experience (and in one's reading of the part's histrionic history) must have wondered why it exists at all. Shakespeare, for once in a way, is entirely to blame. The little scene has no dramatic validity. It sets out to prove that to play a recorder is 'as easy as lying' and it fails to prove this. It proves nothing whatever except that Guildenstern cannot begin to play a recorder, and that Hamlet apparently can! But to what purpose?

Hippolyta in *A Midsummer Night's Dream* (v, i, 122) mentions the same instrument in her criticism of the Prologue to Pyramus and Thisbe. 'Indeed he hath play'd on this prologue like a child on a **recorder**; a sound, but not in government.' Here again it is implied that to play a recorder at all is certainly not 'as easy as lying'. 'In government' means simply 'in tune'.)

       ★   ★   ★

SACKBUTS. These also are obsolete instruments, mentioned only once in the whole of Shakespeare (see under CYMBALS). The sackbut was a wind instrument, a kind of bass instrument with a slide, like that of a trombone, for altering the pitch.

       ★   ★   ★

TABORS AND TABORINES (see also under PIPES). These are forms of drum (quite distinct from the tambour and the tambourine). The tabor was a small drum used chiefly as an accompaniment to the pipe or trumpet.

A tabor is carried by Feste in *Twelfth Night* (III, i, I) when he exchanges some not very witty chop-logic with Viola:

VIOLA: Save thee, friend, and thy music! dost thou live by thy **tabor**?

FESTE: No, sir, I live by the church.

VIOLA: Art thou a churchman?

FESTE: No such matter, sir: I do live by the church; for I do live at my house, and my house doth stand by the church.

VIOLA: So thou mayst say, the king lies by a beggar, if a beggar dwell near him; or, the church stands by thy tabor, if thy tabor stand by the church.

FESTE: You have said, sir.

It is not perhaps the worthiest scene in this delicious play.

It is with a tabor, too, that Ariel in *The Tempest* (IV, i, 175) lures and beguiles the shipwrecked Italians – 'Then I beat my **tabor**' – till they are all standing up to the neck in the waters of a stagnant pool. Perhaps the sprite had been overhearing too much of their laboured persiflage?

Tabourines rattle at the very end of a superb scene in which Antony and Cleopatra do honour to the warrior Scarus for his valour in that day's battle (IV, viii, 22):

ANTONY: Behold this man;
  Commend unto his lips thy favouring hand:—
  Kiss it, my warrior:—he hath fought to-day
  As if a god, in hate of mankind, had
  Destroy'd in such a shape.
CLEOPATRA: I'll give thee, friend,
  An armour all of gold; it was a king's.
ANTONY: He hath deserved it, were it carbuncled
  Like holy Phoebus' car.—Give me thy hand:—
  Through Alexandria make a jolly march;
  Bear our hack'd targets like the men that owe them:
  Had our great palace the capacity
  To camp this host, we all would sup together,
  And drink carouses to the next day's fate,
  Which promises royal peril.—Trumpeters,
  With brazen din blast you the city's ear;
  Make mingle with our rattling **tabourines**;
  That heaven and earth may strike their sounds together,
  Applauding our approach.

★   ★   ★

TRUMPETS (see under CYMBALS and TABORS in this section).
  Trumpets snarl innumerably in the plays:
  'There roar'd the sea, and **trumpet**-clangour sounds.' – Pistol in *King Henry IV, Part Two*, (V, v, 41).
  'The Moor! I know his **trumpet**.' – Iago in *Othello* (II, i, 179).

'What **trumpet's** that?' 'I know't, my sister's.' – Regan in *King Lear* (II, iv, 184).

'**Trumpet**, blow loud. Send thy brass voice through all these lazy tents.' – Aeneas in *Troilus and Cressida* (I, iii, 256).

'Now,—when the angry **trumpet** sounds alarum, and dead men's cries do fill the empty air.' – Warwick at Saint Albans in *King Henry VI, Part Two* (v, ii, 3)—a play which no one, not even the dramatic critics, pretends to know well.

'The **trumpet** sounds retreat; the days is ours.' – Prince Hal in *King Henry IV, Part One* (v, iv, 162).

'By Chrish, la, tish ill done; the work ish given over, the **trompet** sound the retreat.' – Macmorris in *King Henry V* (III, ii, 89).

'Sound drums and **trumpets**, boldly and cheerfully; God and Saint George!' – Richmond in *King Richard III* (v, iii, 270).

'Sound drums and **trumpets**, and the king will fly.' – Richard Plantagenet in *King Henry VI, Part Three* (I, i, 118).

'Sound drums and **trumpets**;—and to London all.' – Warwick in *King Henry VI, Part Two* (v, iii, 32).

These are ten of the many examples. And after all this 'brazen din' (in Mark Antony's phrase) it says much for John Dryden that there is no kind of anti-climax in his poem in honour of St Cecilia's Day in the year 1687, nearly seventy years after Shakespeare's heyday:

> The trumpet's loud clangor
> Excites us to arms,
> With shrill notes of anger
> And mortal alarms.
> The double double double beat
> Of the thundering drum
> Cries, Hark! the foes come;
> Charge, charge, 'tis too late to retreat.

VIOLS AND VIOL-DE-GAMBOYS. The viol – which is the violin's predecessor – is mentioned by Mowbray, Duke of Norfolk, in *King Richard II* in the course of his noble speech on his own banishment from England for evermore. The king has just expressed his fate more characteristically (I, iii, 150).

> The sly slow hours shall not determinate
> The dateless limit of thy dear exile;—
> The hopeless word of 'never to return'
> Breathe I against thee, upon pain of life.

And Mowbray has his eloquent and much less affected reply including the lines (I, iii, 160–62):

> My native English, now I must forgo:
> And now my tongue's use is to me no more
> Than an unstringéd **viol** or a harp; . . .

The viol is again mentioned in *Pericles, Prince of Tyre* (III, ii, 88) as part of the music that brought back to life Queen Thaisa who had been long tossing in the waves in a kind of floating coffin:

> The rough and woeful music that we have,
> Cause it to sound, beseech you.
> The **viol** once more: . . .

And one may still live to see the day when, in a production of *Twelfth Night*, Sir Andrew Aguecheek is seen to take his early violoncello (the viola de gamba) between his knees and play it. For we have Sir Toby Belch's authority (I, iii, 25), expressed to Maria, that the foolish knight 'plays o' th' **viol-de-gamboys**, and speaks three or four languages word for word without book, and hath all the good gifts of nature.'

VIRGINALS. The first English stringed keyboard instrument. When there were two keyboards it was called 'the virginals'. It is known that Queen Elizabeth herself played it, and played it well. It had no legs and when wanted it was placed on a table or a suitable stand.

Shakespeare's sole reference is oblique and curious. This occurs in *The Winter's Tale* (I, ii, 125), where the insanely jealous Leontes is speculating on the possible bastardy of his little son by Hermione, the prince Mamillius. He fumes because Hermione is persuading his friend Polixenes, by means of hand-clasps, to extend his stay. Leontes mutters to himself: 'Still **virginalling** upon his palm?', then turns to the little boy and says aloud: 'How now, you wanton calf! *Art* thou my calf?'

See also under SONGS AND SINGING

SCRAPPING AND WRESTLING

It is odd to find that a 'scrap', in the sense of a fight or tussle between two, is only as old as the year 1874 when it had a slang origin. Shakespeare uses the now-archaic word 'foin' in this sense, especially concerning a fight or scrimmage with pointed weapons. (See also under DUELLING AND FENCING).

Thus in *Part Two* of *King Henry IV* Mistress Quickly says of Falstaff to the sheriff's officers, Fang and Snare (II, I, 12–14): 'Alas the day, take heed of him, he stabbed me in mine own house, most beastly in good faith, 'a cares not what mischief he does, if his weapon be out, he will **foin** like any devil, he will spare neither man, woman, nor child'.

And again, in the same act of the same play, Doll Tearsheet reminds Falstaff of his mortality (II, 4, 222–25): 'Thou whoreson little tidy Bartholomew boar-pig, when wilt thou leave fighting o' days and **foining** o' nights, and begin to patch up thine old body for heaven?' And Doll receives her immortal answer from the old knight: 'Peace, good Doll, do not speak like a death's-head, do not bid me remember mine end.'

There would seem to be no reference to boxing, or fighting

with gloves, anywhere in Shakespeare. Half-a-dozen times
at least a 'box on the ear' is given or taken. Thus Portia
discussing her suitors with her maid Nerissa (in *The Merchant
of Venice*) said of the Scottish lord that he 'borrowed a box
of the ear of the Englishman, and swore he would pay him
back when he was able'. (Editor Ridley in the New Temple
edition drily comments here: 'This would not do for performance before King James.')

Again, in the innermost heart of the unfamiliar trilogy
about the Wars of the Roses, *Part Two* of *King Henry VI*,
we may like to note a colloquy between Lord Say (who is
just about to be beheaded off-stage) and that bloodthirsty
rebel Jack Cade. The rebel has just expressed himself in
admirably clear prose on the subject of his distrust of
education (IV vii 22):

> Well, he shall be beheaded for it ten times. Ah,
> thou say, thou serge, nay, thou buckram lord! now art thou
> within point-blank of our jurisdiction regal . . . I am the besom
> that must sweep the court clean of such filth as
> thou art. Thou has most traitorously corrupted the
> youth of the realm in erecting a grammar school:
> and whereas before, our forefathers had no other books
> but the score and the tally, thou hast caused printing
> to be used, and contrary to the king, his crown and
> dignity, thou hast built a paper-mill. It will be
> proved to thy face thou hast men about thee that usually
> talk of a noun and a verb, and such abominable words
> as no Christian ear can endure to hear . . .

Then Lord Say and Jack Cade have their relevant interchange (IV, vii, 81–82):

SAY: These cheeks are pale for watching for your good.
CADE: Give him a box o' the ear, and that will make them red again.

The word 'boxing' – in the sense of that sport or pastime

[75]

in which two men wearing boxing-gloves exchange blows and parries and feints in accordance with the set rules and for the delectation of onlookers – does not seem to have been in use before the very beginning of the eighteenth century (and therefore a full century after Shakespeare's death).

In Shakespeare this ancient sport of wrestling is almost entirely in the hands (and arms, and legs) of Charles the Wrestler in *As You Like It*. This is the character with whom Orlando tries a fall, and, very surprisingly, wins it to the deep and lasting admiration of Rosalind who is a spectator at the match. The part of Charles is one which depends much more upon physical stamina than upon eloquence, and yet – such is the incalculable nature of the playwright – he is given perhaps the most beautiful little prose-speech (under fifty words) of any minor character in all the works. Usually this is beyond the vocal and expressive powers of the brawny young actor chosen for Charles. But this is what he has to say (I, I, 115):

OLIVER: Where will the old duke live?
CHARLES: They say he is already in the forest of Arden, and a many merry men with him; and there they live like the old Robin Hood of England; they say many young gentlemen flock to him every day, and fleet the time carelessly as they did in the golden world.

Charles has altogether some 350 words of such good prose to speak, at the end of which he is thrown by Orlando, and borne away. He does not reappear in the play, though doubtless he might be recognized as the heftiest of the banished Duke's supporters in the Forest of Arden. No Charles that one can trace ever developed into a celebrated actor, though this is a nice subject for theatrical research through the ages.

A certain celebrated actor, still very much alive, strikingly failed to make a success as Orlando in his youth. The truth is that he very nearly lost the wrestling-match at the beginning of the play. Vividly across the years one remembers him being 'thrown' by an over-enthusiastic Charles the Wrestler, so that he smacked the stage with his shoulders and had some considerable difficulty in getting to his feet again without help.

SHOVEL-BOARD

With a marvellous mixture of sheer good luck and some little skill in plodding research, one can follow an obscure hint in Shakespeare to something like the humble and ubiquitous modern tavern-game of 'shove-ha'penny'. It occurs in a passage-at-arms in the Boar's-Head Tavern in Eastcheap when Falstaff and Pistol seem bent on quarrelling and Doll Tearsheet and Bardolph are at least trying to keep the peace – *King Henry IV, Part Two* (II, iv, 182):

FALSTAFF: Pistol, I would be quiet.

PISTOL: Sweet knight, I kiss thy neif: what! we have seen the seven stars.

DOLL: For God's sake, thrust him down stairs: I cannot endure such a fustian rascal.

PISTOL: Thrust him down stairs! know we not
Galloway nags?

FALSTAFF: Quoit him down, Bardolph, like a **shove-groat shilling**: nay, an a'do nothing but speak nothing, a' shall be nothing here.

BARDOLPH: Come, get you down stairs.

PISTOL: What! shall we have incision? shall we imbrue?—

[he snatches up his sword

Then death rock me asleep, abridge my doleful days!
Why, then, let grievous, ghastly, gaping wounds
Untwine the Sisters Three! Come, Atropos, I say!

[he offers to fight

HOSTESS: Here's goodly stuff toward!

Goodly stuff indeed, but far from easy with its many allusions to old plays and forgotten ballads!

We know that 'neif' or 'nieve' means 'hand' or 'fist', that it is also used by Bottom the Weaver and Robert Burns in that sense, and that it is still current in Scottish dialect where it nowadays means a *clenched* fist. We know too that 'Galloway nags' are the little horses peculiar to south-west Scotland.

But Falstaff's 'Quoit him down, Bardolph, like a shovegroat shilling' is the exciting line that gives us pause. 'Quoit' here means simply 'strike' or 'pitch', and 'shove-groat shilling' clearly implies the shoving of a coin of sorts, hence shovel-board. Editor Hudson tells us that *shove-groat shillings* were broad shillings of King Edward VI. In *The Merry Wives of Windsor* they are spoken of as *Edward shovel-boards.*' We turn the pages and find there (I, i, 144):

FALSTAFF: Pistol, did you pick Master Slender's purse?
SLENDER: Ay, by these gloves, did he ... of seven groats in millsixpences, and two Edward **shovel-boards**, that cost me two shilling and two pence a-piece of Yead Miller, by these gloves.

And in his note to the passage Editor Hudson is again most helpful: '*Milled*, or *stamped*, sixpences were used as *counters*; said to have been first coined in 1561.—Edward *shovel-boards* were the broad shillings of Edward VI, used for playing the game of *shuffle-board*; the shilling being placed on the edge of the table, and driven at the mark by a stroke of the hand.'

And my old Fleet Street colleague, Mr Vernon Bartlett, is more helpful still in his recent book, *The Past of Pastimes*: ' "Shovel-board" was a large-scale variety of that splendid public house game, shove ha'penny, ... [It] is played on a small board of hardwood or slate on a pub table, and its antiquity is indicated by the fact that it was formerly known as "shove groat" or "slyp groat". .... Say what you will, there is a certain beauty about the gentleness with which some farm labourer with a fist like a sledge-hammer will nudge his coin into the proper "bed" with the palm of his hand.'

It may round off this little exercise if we finally point out that the boy-king Edward VI died in 1553, eleven years before Shakespeare was born.

SONGS and SINGING

AIRS. 'Now, divine **air**! now is his soul ravish'd!' Thus Benedick, while the musicians play the air Balthazar is about to sing in *Much Ado About Nothing* (II, iii, 60). And he goes on: 'Is it not strange that sheeps' guts should hale souls out of men's bodies?' Across the years – nearly fifty of them now – one remembers the hum of appreciation, a kind of audible smile, that went through the audience when the Benedick of Henry Ainley uttered this whimsey. The song that follows is 'Sigh no more, ladies'.

The oafish Cloten, with that occasional lyrical tone to his rough tongue, has a very similar remark in *Cymbeline* (II, iii, 19). This concerns that abstruse play's beautiful song, 'Hark, hark! the lark', which he preludes with the line: 'A wonderful sweet **air**, with admirable rich words to it.' He follows the song's performance with some further words to the musicians (II, iii, 30): 'So, get you gone. If this penetrate [to Imogen], I will consider your music the better: if it do not, it is a vice in her ears, which horse-hairs and calves'-guts, nor the voice of unpaved eunuch to boot, can never amend.'

★   ★   ★

ANTHEMS. One of the Two Gentlemen of Verona (Valentine) asks the other one (Proteus) for a word of comfort in his sorrows – 'as ending **anthem** of my endless dolour' (III, i, 240).

And Falstaff, in *King Henry IV, Part Two* (I, ii, 194), protests to the Lord Chief Justice that he is not nearly so old as he looks and sounds: 'For my voice,—I have lost it with hallooing, and singing of **anthems**.'

BALLADS. Shakespeare is bounteous with mention of actual ballads (existing or lost), most especially in *The Winter's Tale*, where Autolycus sells them among his knick-knacks. But none of these has anything like the suggestive allurement of the story begun by little Prince Mamillius in the same play, a tale 'of sprites and goblins' of which, maddeningly, we possess nothing but the very first line: 'There was a man, dwelt by a churchyard' (II, i, 29).

There is one mention of ballad-makers in a remarkable colloquy between the serving-men of Aufidius in *Coriolanus*. The lines are seldom heard in the theatre because they are usually cut from any performance. But the colloquy is worth studying if only for its unusual pro-war trend. It concludes thus (IV, v, 202), and the discussion, of course, concerns Coriolanus himself:

THIRD SERV.: . . . he has as many friends as enemies: which friends, sir, as it were, durst not, look you, sir, show themselves, as we term it, his friends whilst he's in directitude.

FIRST SERV.: Directitude! what's that?

THIRD SERV.: But when they shall see, sir, his crest up again, and the man in blood, they will out of their burrows, like conies after rain, and revel all with him.

FIRST SERV.: But when goes this forward?

THIRD SERV.: To-morrow; to-day; presently; you shall have the drum struck up this afternoon: 'tis, as it were, a parcel of their feast, and to be executed ere they wipe their lips.

SECOND SERV.: Why, then we shall have a stirring world again. This peace is nothing, but to rust iron, increase tailors, and breed **ballad-makers.**

FIRST SERV.: Let me have war, say I; it exceeds peace as far as day does night; it's spritely, waking, audible, and full of vent [= pluck and courage]. Peace is a very apoplexy, lethargy; mull'd, deaf, sleepy, insensible; a getter of more bastard children than war's a destroyer of men.

SECOND SERV.: 'Tis so: and as war, in some sort, may be said to be a ravisher, so it cannot be denied but peace is a great maker of cuckolds.

FIRST SERV.: Ay, and it makes men hate one another.

THIRD SERV.: Reason; because they then less need one another. The wars for my money. I hope to see Romans as cheap as Volscians.— They are rising, they are rising.

ALL THREE: In, in, in, in!

They have points of view, and express them racily. It is stupid as well as snobbish to cut them entirely.

★   ★   ★

CATCHES. A catch, or round in which each singer echoes the one before, producing light-hearted or comical effects, is a word which would seem to have been brand-new when Shakespeare introduced it in his *Twelfth Night* around the year 1600.

Feste has just delivered himself of the song 'O mistress mine', when Sir Toby says: 'But shall we make the welkin dance indeed? shall we rouse the night-owl in a **catch** that will draw three souls out of one weaver? shall we do that?' And Sir Andrew agrees: 'An you love me, let's do't: I am dog at a **catch**. . . . Let our **catch** be, "Thou knave."' (II, iii, 56). They set about it. Then Malvolio comes in to quieten the roysterers: 'My masters, are you mad? or what are you? Have you no wit, manners, nor honesty, but to gabble like tinkers at this time of night? Do you make an ale-house of my lady's house, that ye squeak out your coziers' **catches** without any mitigation or remorse of voice?' And Sir Toby rudely answers the pompous Puritan: 'We did keep time, sir, in our **catches**. Sneck-up!' (II, iii, 84). It is as though the players could not utter the new word often enough. The catch was the catch-word of the season.

Some other quite elemental characters – Caliban and his new friends, Trinculo and Stephano – also prove themselves dogs at a catch – in *The Tempest* (III, ii, 118):

CALIBAN: Thou makest me merry; I am full of pleasure:
  Let us be jocund: will you troll the **catch**
  You taught me but while-ere?
STEPHANO: At thy request, monster, I will do reason, any reason.—
  Come on, Trinculo, let us sing.
  'Flout 'em and scout 'em,' etc.
CALIBAN: That's not the tune.

There follows the stage-direction: '*Ariel plays a tune on a tabor and pipe*', and the scene goes on magically to its celebrated climax:

STEPHANO: What is this same?
TRINCULO: This is the tune of our **catch**, played by the picture of
  Nobody.
STEPHANO: If thou be'st a man, show thyself in thy likeness: if thou
  be'st a devil, take't as thou list.
TRINCULO: O, forgive me my sins!
STEPHANO: He that dies pays all debts: I defy thee.—
  Mercy upon us!
CALIBAN: Art thou afeard?
STEPHANO: No, monster, not I.
CALIBAN: Be not afeard; the isle is full of noises,
  Sounds, and sweet airs, that give delight, and hurt not.
  Sometimes a thousand twangling instruments
  Will hum about mine ears; and sometimes voices,
  That, if I then had waked after long sleep,
  Will make me sleep again: and then, in dreaming,
  The clouds methought would open, and show riches
  Ready to drop upon me; that, when I waked,
  I cried to dream again. . . .

           ★   ★   ★

DITTIES. It is a carefree-sounding word. But an odd majority of those mentioned or quoted by Shakespeare are melancholy. 'It was a lover and his lass' in *As You Like It* is sung in good cheer by two Pages, but it meets with a jarring note in Touchstone's criticism (v, iii, 33):

TOUCHSTONE: Truly, young gentlemen, though there was no great matter in the **ditty**, yet the note was very untuneable.

FIRST PAGE: You are deceived, sir: we kept time, we lost not our time.

TOUCHSTONE: By my troth, yes; I count it but time lost to hear such a foolish song. God b'wi'you; and God mend your voices!— Come, Audrey.

One rejoices to see that the performers answered the self-appointed music-critic – with right and justice, apart from a not unimportant misunderstanding between 'keeping time' and 'keeping in tune'.

In *Much Ado About Nothing* (II, iii, 73) the famous song which begins 'Sigh no more, ladies' goes on to ask them further:

> Sing no more **ditties**, sing no moe
> Of dumps so dull and heavy. . . .

In *King Henry IV, Part One* (III, i, 120) that consummate Welshman, Owen Glendower, tells Hotspur:

> I can speak English, lord, as well as you;
> For I was train'd up in the English court;
> Where, being but young, I framed to the harp
> Many an English **ditty** lovely well, . . .

And later in the same scene Mortimer, Earl of March, says to his own Welsh-speaking lady (III, i, 202):

> I understand thy kisses, and thou mine,
> And that's a feeling disputation:
> But I will never be a truant, love,
> Till I have learn'd thy langyage; for thy tongue
> Makes Welsh as sweet as **ditties** newly penn'd,
> Sung by a fair queen in a summer's bower,
> With ravishing division, to her lute.

And twenty lines or so later Hotspur has an interchange with his own Welsh-speaking wife which Eric Partridge in his immensely suggestive book, *Shakespeare's Bawdy*, convinces us to be very sexual indeed in its double-meanings:

HOTSPUR: Come, Kate, thou art perfect in lying down: come, quick, quick, quick, that I may lay my head in thy lap.
LADY PERCY: Go, ye giddy goose.   [*The music plays*
HOTSPUR: Now I perceive the devil understands Welsh;
And 'tis no marvel he is so humorous.
By'r lady, he is a good musician.
LADY PERCY: Then should you be nothing but musical; for you are altogether govern'd by humours. Lie still, ye thief, and hear the lady **sing** in Welsh.

One well remembers the grace and beauty – positively Welsh in its intensity and fun – of Margaret Leighton as Lady Percy. She had that prince of Hotspurs, Olivier, very much with her. It was the great season when the Old Vic was at the New Theatre; and Ralph Richardson was the glorious Falstaff in this same play; and the war was ended, and it seemed that civilization had begun all over again.

★   ★   ★

HYMNS. A hymn is, according to the dictionary, a solemn song to God or some lesser deity. (It can therefore be both ancient and modern.) All of Shakespeare's references are intensely poetical.

Capulet on Juliet's death ordains (*Romeo and Juliet*, IV, v, 88): 'Our solemn **hymns** to sullen dirges change.'

Lorenzo at Belmont orders a hymn to be sung for the return of Portia (*The Merchant of Venice*, V, i, 66): 'Come, ho, and wake Diana with a **hymn**!' and Jessica, a shade unnecessarily replies, that she is never merry when she hears such sweet music.

In *A Midsummer Night's Dream* (I, i, 73) Theseus tells Hermia that, if she chooses not to marry, she may for the rest of her life have to be 'chanting faint **hymns** to the cold fruitless moon' (observe the loaded meaning of the word 'fruitless'). And in the same play Titania, in the course of a lovely forty-lines-long speech on the disorders in Nature caused by her quarrel with Oberon has the line (ɪɪ, i, 102): 'No night is now with **hymn** or carol blest.'

Claudio in *Much Ado About Nothing* (v, iii, 11) has the effrontery to give an order to the chorus at Hero's mockfuneral: 'Now, music, sound, and sing your solemn **hymn**.'

And Shakespeare himself, presumably, in the Sonnets (No. 29, lines 10–12) describes how he can soar out of unhappiness:

> Haply I think on thee,—and then my state,
> Like to the lark at break of day arising
> From sullen earth, sings **hymns** at heaven's gate; . . .

*   *   *

TUNES. Of all the kings in Shakespeare the least satisfactory and most inconsequent is surely Cymbelina, whose only two virtues are (1) that he gave his name to one of Shakespeare's least satisfactory and most inconsistent plays and (2) that at least he was the father of that most satisfactory and consistent of heroines, the princess Imogen.

And of the whole part of Cymbeline himself, only a single line – which is only half a line – is glowing with poetry. It is in the scene (*Cymbeline*, v, v, 236) in which Imogen confronts Pisanio whom she suspects of having tried to poison her, and accuses him in the presence of the king himself with the words:

> O, get thee from my sight;
> Thou gavest me poison: dangerous fellow, hence!
> Breathe not where princes are.

It is a proud and flashing utterance (to which Ellen Terry's famous Imogen must have done justice). And Cymbeline's half-line of comment is a sudden ecstatic appreciation of his radiant daughter. It is of six syllables only, but they are a little poem in purest music. They are the words: 'The **tune** of Imogen!'

SWIMMING

There is far more swimming done in *The Tempest* than in any other of the plays. Ariel can obviously swim like a fish as well as fly like a bat or a swallow, and he says so in an entreaty to Prospero to command him anything (i, ii, 189):

> All hail, great master! grave sir, hail! I come
> To answer thy best pleasure; be't to fly,
> To **swim**, to dive into the fire, to ride
> On the curl'd clouds,—to thy strong bidding task
> Ariel and all his quality.

And both Stephano and Trinculo in the same play tell us that they swim like ducks and better than geese.

Every schoolboy remembers how Cassius was challenged by Julius Caesar to swim in the Tiber (i, ii, 100) and how he describes the incident to Brutus long afterwards:

> For once, upon a raw and gusty day,
> The troubled Tiber chasing with her shores,
> Caesar said to me, 'Dare'st thou, Cassius, now
> Leap in with me into this angry flood,
> And **swim** to yonder point?' Upon the word,
> Accoutred as I was, I plungèd in,
> And bade him follow: so, indeed, he did.
> The torrent roar'd; and we did buffet it
> With lusty sinews, throwing it aside
> And stemming it with hearts of controversy;
> But ere we could arrive the point proposed,
> Caesar cried, 'Help me, Cassius, or I sink!' . . .

And the Fool says expressively to King Lear, when the latter tears off his clothes in the storm (*King Lear*, iii, iv, 113): 'Prithee, nuncle, be contented; 'tis a naughty night to **swim** in.'

TENNIS

Shakespeare's references to the game of bowls are much more frequent and detailed than those to tennis, and it is probably rightly argued that the former was what he greatly preferred above all other ball-games.

But the allusion to tennis-balls in *King Henry V* (I, ii, 235–99) must give us particular pause, especially as neither Dr Caroline Spurgeon (1935) nor Mr Eric Partridge in *Shakespeare's Bawdy* (1947) makes any mention of them. A chestful of tennis-balls is sent as a present from the Dauphin of France to the King of England, and it is not possible at this time of day. They arrive as **balls**, *tout court* and unqualified, and that they were meant as a direct insult is perfectly clear from the text. One gives here the Olivier film-text, but though transposed it is unaltered:

Enter Ambassadors of France

KING HENRY: Now are we well prepared to know the pleasure
   Of our fair cousin Dauphin; for we hear
   Your greeting is from him, not from the king.
AMBASSADOR: May't please your majesty to give us leave
   Freely to render what we have in charge;
   Or shall we sparingly show you far off
   The Dauphin's meaning and our embassy?
KING HENRY: We are no tyrant, but a Christian king; . . .
   Therefore with frank and with uncurbed plainness
   Tell us the Dauphin's mind.
AMBASSADOR: Thus, then, in few.
   Your highness, lately sending into France,
   Did claim some certain dukedoms, in the right
   Of your great predecessor, King Edward the Third.
   In answer of which claim, the prince our master
   Says, that you savour too much of your youth; . . .
   He therefore sends you, meeter for your spirit,

This tun of treasure; and, in lieu of this,
 Desires you let the kingdoms that you claim
 Hear no more of you. This the Dauphin speaks.
KING HENRY: What treasure, uncle?
DUKE OF EXETER: **Tennis-balls**, my liege.
KING HENRY: We are glad the Dauphin is so pleasant with us;
 His present and your pains, we thank you for:
 When we have match'd our **rackets** to these **balls**,
 We will, in France, by God's grace, play a **set**
 Shall strike his father's crown into the hazard. . . .
 And tell the pleasant prince, this mock of his
 Hath turn'd his **balls** to gun-stones, and his soul
 Shall stand sore charged for the wasteful vengeance
 That shall fly with them: for many a thousand widows
 Shall this his mock mock out of their dear husbands;
 Mock mothers from their sons, mock castles down;
 And, some are yet ungotten and unborn
 That shall have cause to curse the Dauphin's scorn. . . .
 So, get you hence in peace; and tell the Dauphin,
 His jest will savour but of shallow wit,
 When thousands weep, more than did laugh at it.
 Convey them with safe conduct.—Fare you well.

[Exeunt Ambassadors

All who saw the film must well remember the long pause
immediately after Exeter's 'Tennis-balls, my liege', and then
the mounting rage and speed of the Olivier Henry thereafter
– with, all the while, a chest full of offensive white tennis-balls
in full view of everybody throughout the episode.

 Later on in the play Exeter has a colloquy with the Dauphin
and the French King, when the subject is raised again (II, 3,
127–140):
DAUPHIN: Say, if my father render fair return,
 It is against my will; for I desire
 Nothing but odds with England: to that end
 As matching to his youth and vanity,
 I did present him with the Paris **balls**.

EXETER: He'll make your Paris Louvre shake for it
  Were it the mistress Court of mighty Europe:
  And be assured you'll find a difference,
  As we his subjects have in wonder found
  Between the promise of his greener days
  And there he masters now: now he weighs time,
  Even to the utmost grain: that you shall read
  In your own losses if he stay in France.
FRENCH KING: To-morrow shall you know our mind at full.

It is all very mettlesome and eloquent. But it is also an example of periphrasis – i.e. saying in many words what a single short word (familiar in to-day's colloquial English) would express. Shakespeare's historical authority the chronicler Holinshed, is no less periphrastic in his way and in his quaint old spelling:

Whilest in the Lent season the king laie at Killingworth, there came to him from Charles Dolphin of France certeine ambassadors, that brought with them a barrell of Paris *balles* [the italics are Holinshed's]; which from their meister they presented to him for a token that was taken in verie ill part, as sent in scorne, to signifie, that it was more meet for the king to passe the time with such childish exercise, than to attempt any worthie exploit.

WALKING

Walking for no other purpose than exercise is fairly infrequent in the plays. Gloucester in *King Henry VI, Part Two* (I, iii, 150) deliberately walks himself into a good temper:

> Now, lords, my choler being over-blown
> With **walking** once about the quadrangle,
> I come to talk of commonwealth affairs. . . .

There is an extremely odd little scene in *Macbeth* (III, vi) of some fifty lines in all, which has two references to Banquo's habit of 'walking too late', and so much else beside of mysterious interest and power that one has no hesitation whatever in giving it here in its inexplicable entirety. The scene tells us a little, though not enough, about the baffling character called Lennox, and it tells us just as little about the only other character in the scene, who is a Lord without even a name. The scene, set in the king's palace at Forres, is oddly placed between two meetings of the Witches – the rarely played Hecate scene and the Cauldron scene (both sometimes attributed, at least in part, to Middleton rather than Shakespeare).

Let us quote it complete, before asking further about its significance, and let us note while reading it that almost every line of it gives us pause for wonderment at the sincerity of the speaker, whether it be Lennox or the Lord:

LENNOX: My former speeches have but hit your thoughts,
   Which can interpret further: only, I say,
   Things have been strangely borne. The gracious Duncan
   Was pitied of Macbeth:—marry, he was dead:—
   And the right-valiant Banquo **walk'd** too late;
   Whom, you may say, if't please you, Fleance kill'd,
   For Fleance fled: men must not **walk** too late.
   Who cannot want the thought, how monstrous
   It was for Malcolm and for Donalbain
   To kill their gracious father? damned fact!
   How it did grieve Macbeth! did he not straight,
   In pious rage, the two delinquents **tear,**
   That were the slaves of drink and thralls of sleep?
   Was not that nobly done? Ay, and wisely too;
   For 'twould have anger'd any heart alive
   To hear the men deny't. So that, I say,
   He has borne all things well: and I do think
   That, had he Duncan's sons under his key,—
   As, an't please heaven, he shall not,—they should find
   What 'twere to kill a father; so should Fleance.

But, peace!—for from broad words, and 'cause he fail'd
His presence at the tyrant's feast, I hear,
Macduff lives in disgrace: sir, can you tell
Where he bestows himself?

LORD: The son of Duncan,
From whom this tyrant holds the due of birth,
Lives in the English court; and is received
Of the most pious Edward with such grace,
That the malevolence of fortune nothing
Takes from his high respect: thither Macduff
Is gone to pray the holy king, upon his aid
To wake Northumberland and warlike Siward:
That, by the help of these—with Him above
To ratify the work—we may again
Give to our tables meat, sleep to our nights;
Free from our feasts and banquets bloody knives;
Do faithful homage, and receive free honours;—
All which we pine for now: and this report
Hath so exasperate the king, that he
Prepares for some attempt of war.

LENNOX: Sent he to Macduff?

LORD: He did: and with an absolute 'Sir, not I',
The cloudy messenger turns me his back,
And hums; as who should say, 'You'll rue the time
That clogs me with this answer.'

LENNOX: And that well might
Advise him to a caution, to hold what distance
His wisdom can provide. Some holy angel
Fly to the court of England, and unfold
His message ere he come; that a swift blessing
May soon return to this our suffering country
Under a hand accurst!

LORD: I'll send my prayers with him.

This may be called Lennox's single scene. He has only a
line or two more to utter – though they are usually lines well
worth uttering. At his very first appearance in the play he

has to speak about that no less cryptic character, Ross, the quite astonishing two lines (I, ii, 47–8):

> What a haste looks through his eyes! So should he look
> That seems to speak things strange.

Later (IV, i, 139) Lennox has a brief colloquy with Macbeth himself just after the latter has again interviewed the Witches:

MACBETH: I did hear
  The galloping of horse: who was't came by?
LENNOX: 'Tis two or three, my lord, that bring you word
  Macduff is fled to England.
MACBETH: Fled to England!
LENNOX: Ay, my good lord.

John Masefield, finely imaginative as a critic as well as a poet, says of this: 'An echo of the galloping stays in the brain, as though the hoofs of some horse rode the night, carrying away Macbeth's luck for ever.' No less superbly and in the same essay he answers the current cliché question as to what *Macbeth* is all *about*: – '[it] is about the desecration of the holiness of human life.'

If all this should seem to be taking us very far away from the pastime of walking, whether by day or by night, and whether for exercise or for relaxation, let us easily revert to it by way of Prospero in *The Tempest*. This old or ageing magician – in whom it is possible, without any great stretch of imagination, to recognize the great creative poet himself nearing the end of his enterprise – proposes to take a walk up and down in order to still his 'beating mind' (IV, i, 161).

He might well. Not only has he been conjuring visions and masques to entertain his daughter Miranda and her chosen Ferdinand. But he has also recollected a conspiracy being waged against him, just before delivering himself of twelve lines of farewell, unsurpassed for ache and quiet beauty. These done – and they have to be breathed as Gielgud breathes them – old Prospero descends from the superhuman to the human again, and sends the young people in to rest, and says he must walk a little in order to recover and refresh himself. To still his 'beating mind'!

Rosalind in *As You Like It* and Imogen in *Cymbeline* are perhaps the most practised walkers in the whole of Shakespeare. They are both not at all unlike the strapping heroines of George Meredith nearly three centuries later – Lucy and Clare in *Feverel*, Rhoda and Dahlia Fleming, Diana and Carinthia. These Meredithian ladies were, in their turn, affectionately parodied by Max Beerbohm in the hefty Euphemia Clashthought (a piece of nomenclature which is in itself an inspired piece of parody or literary caricature).

In order to send the reader back to the joys of Max's *Christmas Garland*, one should only have to quote the last paragraph in the last parody of that ineffable collection. Euphemia, on a Sunday morning in the snowbound countryside, gazes upon her fiancé Sir Rebus, somnolent beside a decanter of old port. She suddenly decides to leave him there and go for a solitary long walk – perhaps because it seems the Meredithian thing to do:

'Mother Earth, white-mantled, called to her. Casting eye of caution at recumbence, she paddled across the carpet and anon swam out over the snow. Pagan young womanhood, six foot of it, spanned eight miles before luncheon.'

WAR-MAKING

There is certainly as much of war as there is of peace in the entire output of Shakespeare – as much about discord as there is about concord. It does not follow, by any manner of means, that Shakespeare was a bloody-minded man, simply because he makes Othello speak nobly of war (III, iii, 355) in the volcanic outburst when he tells us that jealousy makes him leave behind his tranquillity and contentment:

> Farewell the plumèd troop, and the big **wars**
> That make ambition virtue! O, farewell,
> Farewell the neighing steed, th' ear-piercing fife,
> The royal banner, and all quality,
> Pride, pomp, and circumstance of glorious **war**!

Shakespeare in himself is no more Othello – or Coriolanus or Hotspur or Achilles, or Mark Antony – than he is that boy-soldier without a name in *King Henry V* who gets battle-scared before Harfleur, and says straight from the heart (III, I, 43): – 'Would I were in an alehouse in London! I would give all my fame for a pot of ale and safety.'

Shakespeare is just as interested in this common soldier as he is in his uncommon heroes, and we may quote more of the Boy here since he is usually cut to ribbons in the theatre (III, I, 60–75):

As young as I am, I have observed these three swashers, I am boy to them all three; but all they three, although they would serve me, could not be man to me; for, indeed, three such antics do not amount to a man. For Bardolph, he is white-liver'd and red-fac'd; by the means whereof he faces it out, but fights not. For Pistol, he hath a killing tongue and a quiet sword: by the means whereof he breaks words, and keeps whole weapons. For Nym, he hath heard that men of few words are the best [= bravest] men; and therefore he scorns to say his prayers, lest he should be thought a coward; but his few bad words are match'd with as few good deeds; for he never broke any man's head but his own, and that was against a post when he was drunk. They will steal any thing, and call it purchase. Bardolph stole a lute-case, bore it twelve leagues, and sold it for three-halfpence. Nym and Bardolph are sworn brothers in filching; and in Calais they stole a fire-shovel: I knew by that piece of service the men would carry coals [= *do the basest things*]. They would have me as familiar with men's pockets as their gloves or their handkerchers: which makes much against my manhood, if I should take from another's pocket to put into mine; for it is plain pocketing-up of wrongs, I must leave them, and seek some better service: their villany goes against my weak stomach, and therefore I must cast it up.

It might be possible to grade the plays of Shakespeare in descending order of the amount of war-making they contain. First, undoubtedly, would come the three parts of *King Henry VI*. Even more than the other histories these are – in Iago's phrase – 'horribly stuffed with epithets of war'. (The three parts have been ingeniously welded into a single viable play by the director John Barton and with the title *The Wars of the Roses*).

Our first illustrating passage is from Part One (II, 4, 107–134):

PLANTAGENET: Now, by my soul, this pale and angry rose,
　　As cognizance of my blood-drinking hate,
　　Will I for ever, and my faction, wear,
　　Until it wither with me to my grave,
　　Or flourish to the height of my degree.
SUFFOLK: Go forward, and be choked with thy ambition!
　　And so, farewell, until I meet thee next.
SOMERSET: Have with thee, Pole.—Farewell, ambitious Richard.
PLANTAGENET: How am I braved, and must perforce endure it!
WARWICK: This blot that they object against our house,
　　Shall be wiped out in the next Parliament,
　　Call'd for the truce of Winchester and Gloster:
　　And if thou be not then created York,
　　I will not live to be accounted Warwick.
　　Meantime, in signal of my love to thee,
　　Against proud Somerset and William Pole,
　　Will I upon thy party wear this rose:
　　And here I prophesy,—this brawl to-day,
　　Grown to this faction, in the Temple Garden,
　　Shall send between the red rose and the white,
　　A thousand souls to death and deadly night.

[95]

PLANTAGENET: Good Master Vernon, I am bound to you,
That you on my behalf would pluck a flower.
VERNON: On your behalf still will I wear the same.
LAUYER: And so will I.
PLANTAGENET: Thanks, gentle sir,
Come, let us four to dinner. I dare say
This quarrel will drink blood another day.

From Part Two of *King Henry VI* (III, 2, 160) comes this bloody scene:

(*The folding-doors of an inner chamber are thrown open, and Gloster is discovered dead in his bed; Warwick and others standing by it.*) . . .

WARWICK: See how the blood is settled in his face!
Oft have I seen a timely-parted ghost,
Of ashy semblance, meagre, pale and bloodless,
Being all descended to the labouring heart;
Who, in the conflict that it holds with death,
Attracts the same for aidance 'gainst the enemy;
Which with the heart there cools, and ne'er returneth
To blush and beautify the cheek again.
But see, his faces is black and full of blood
His eyeballs further out than when he lived,
Staring full ghastly like a strangled man;
His hair uprear'd, his nostrils stretch'd with struggling,
His hands abroad display'd, as one that grasp'd
And tugg'd for life, and was by strength subdued;
Look, on the sheets his hair, you see, is sticking;
His well-proportioned beard made rough and rugged,
Like to the summer's corn by tempest lodged.
It cannot be but he was murder'd here;
The least of all these signs were probable.

And barely thirty lines later, we have this no less sanguinary interchange (III, 2, 210):

SUFFOLK: Blunt-witted lord, ignoble in demeanour!
If ever lady wrong'd her lord so much,

Thy mother took unto her blameful bed
Some stern untutor'd churl, and noble stock
Was graft with crab-tree slip; whose fruit thou art,
And never of the Nevilles' noble race.

WARWICK: But that the guilt of murder bucklers thee,
And I should rob the deathsman of his foe,
Quitting thee thereby of ten thousand shames,
And that my sovereign's presence makes me mild,
I would, false murderous coward, on thy knee
Make thee beg pardon for thy passèd speech,
And say it was thy mother that thou meant'st,—
That thou thyself wast born in bastardy,
And, after all this fearful homage done,
Give thee thy hire, and send thy soul to hell,
Pernicious blood-sucker of sleeping men!

In Part Three of *King Henry VI* (II, 3, 14) we have this
from RICHARD DUKE OF YORK (father of Gloucester later
to become King Richard III):

Ah, Warwick, why hast thou withdrawn thyself?
Thy brother's blood the thirsty earth hath drunk,
Broach'd with the steely point of Clifford's lance;
And, in the very pangs of death, he cried
Like to a dismal clangor heard from far,
'Warwick, revenge! brother, revenge my death!'
So, underneath the belly of their steeds,
That stain'd their fetlocks in his smoking blood,
The noble gentleman gave up the ghost.

And Warwick's reply which is no less bloodthirsty (II, 3, 23):

Then let the earth be drunken with our blood:
I'll kill my horse because I will not fly.
Why stand we like soft-hearted women here,
Wailing our losses, whiles the foe doth rage,
And look upon, as if the tragedy
Were play'd in jest, by counterfeiting actors?

> Here on my knee I vow to God above,
> I'll never pause again, never stand still,
> Till either death hath closed these eyes of mine,
> Or fortune given me measure of revenge.

Professor Edward Dowden, doing his best work one hundred years ago and at one time frequently quoted, is now much out of fashion. But like many another Shakespearean scholar he is likely to emerge from his temporary eclipse. He is particularly good and suggestive on the three parts of *King Henry VI* which so many of the pundits have tended to ignore as being merely Shakespeare's prentice-work:

Among his 'wolfish Earls' Henry is in constant terror, not of himself being torn to pieces, but of their flying at one another's throats. Violent scenes, disturbing the cloistral peace which it would please him to see reign throughout the universe, are hateful and terrible to Henry. He rides out hawking with his Queen and Suffolk, the Cardinal and Gloster; some of the riders hardly able for an hour to conceal their emulation and their hate. Henry takes a languid interest in the sport, but all occasions supply food for his contemplative piety; he suffers from a certain incontinence of devout feeling, and now the falcons set him moralising. A moment after, and the peers, with Margaret among them, are bandying furious words. Henry's anguish is extreme, but he hopes that something may be done by a few moral reflections suitable to the occasion.

In *King Richard III* (v, 3, 328) Richard's himself again, especially before Bosworth Field:

> Let's whip these stragglers o'er the seas again;
> Lash hence these overweening rags of France,
> These famish'd beggars, weary of their lives;
> Who, but for dreaming on this fond exploit,
> For want of means, poor rats, had hang'd themselves.
> If we be conquered, let man conquer us,
> And not these bastard Bretons; whom our fathers
> Have in their own land beaten, bobb'd, and thump'd,

And, on record, left them the heirs of shame.
Shall these enjoy our lands? lie with our wives?
Ravish our daughters? Hark! I hear their drum—
Fight, gentlemen of England! Fight, bold yeomen!
Draw archers, draw your arrows to the head!
Spur your proud horses hard, and ride in blood;
Amaze the welkin with your broken staves.

In *King Richard II* – and especially in the character of Boling-broke (III, 3, 31–48) – the tempest in the blood is again high:

BOLINGBROKE: ... Noble lords,
(*To Northumberland*): Go to the rude ribs of that ancient castle;
  Through brazen trumpet send the breath of parley,
  Into his ruin'd ears, and thus deliver:
  Henry Bolingbroke
  On both his knees doth kiss King Richard's hand,
  And sends allegiance and truth faith of heart
  To his most royal person; hither come
  Even at his feet to lay my arms and power,
  Provided that, my banishment repeal'd,
  And lands restored again, be freely granted:
  If not, I'll use the advantage of my power
  And lay the summer's dust with showers of blood
  Rain'd from the wounds of slaughter'd Englishmen;
  The which, how far off from the mind of Bolingbroke
  It is, such crimson tempest should bedrench
  The fresh green lap of fair King Richard's land,
  My stooping duty tenderly shall show ...

In *King John* the subject of war is handled with a kind of sinister gusto, and nowhere more than in this speech of Falconbridge (II, 1, 456–467), which is only one of many such:

PHILIP FALCONBRIDGE,
  THE BASTARD: Here's a flaw [= gust]
  That shakes the rotten carcass of old Death,
  Out of his rags. Here's a large mouth, indeed,

That spits forth death and mountains, rocks and seas;
Talks as familiarly of roaring lions
As maids of thirteen do of puppy-dogs!
What cannoneer begot this lusty blood?
He speaks plain cannon fire, and smoke, and bounce;
He gives the bastinado with his tongue;
Our ears are cudgell'd; not a word of his
But buffets better than a fist of France:
Zounds, I was never so bethump'd with words
Since I first called my brother's father dad.

Those of us who saw *King Henry IV Part One* and *Part Two* playing alternately in the 1945 Old Vic production at the New Theatre will never forget them; and will indeed regard them as the supreme theatrical experience of the middle of this century. They first began at the end of September and the beginning of October of that year which brought the end of the Second World War.

England was staggered with relief at the lifted burden of the war. And here was Shakespeare's supreme double-play of war and peace. Here was Richardson, superlative as the Falstaff of both Parts. Here was Olivier as Hotspur in Part One, and as Justice Shallow in Part Two – a marvellously contrasted double of fiery youth and crabbed age. Here were Nicholas Hannen's ageing King and Sybil Thorndike's ageless Mistress Quickly. Here were Joyce Redman's frank Doll Tearsheet, and Margaret Leighton's beautifully tolerant and tender Lady Percy. No circumstances can ever again arise to make the double play seem more right, more Shakespearean; and though it is now nearly thirty years since Roger Furse's royal-blue drop-curtain, emblemed with swans, first rose upon the play so richly presented we have often – in the mind's eye – seen it rise again to disclose such majesty and riot.

In *Part One* we need only quote Hotspur at his most martial (v, 2, 92–100):

[100]

> Let each man do his best: and here draw I
> A sword, whose temper I intend to stain
> With the best blood that I can meet withal
> In the adventure of this perilous day.
> Now, Esperance! Percy! and set on,
> Sound all the lofty instruments of **war,**
> And by the music let us all embrace;
> For, heaven to earth, some of us never shall
> A second time to such a courtesy.
> *(The trumpets sound)*

In *Part Two* we need only give Doll Tearsheet's farewell
to Falstaff (II, 4, 60–62):

> Come, I'll be friends with thee, Jack:
> thou art going to the **wars**; and whether
> I shall ever see thee again or no, there
> is nobody cares.

But if we seek peace rather than war in this great double
play, there is peace in plenty at Gadshill in the First Part, in
Gloucestershire in the Second, and in the Boar's Head in
Eastcheap in both.

A colloquy between Falstaff and the jealous Ford (disguising
himself as Master Brook) comes nearer to strife than anything
else in *The Merry Wives of Windsor* (II, 2, 204):

FORD: Now, Sir John, here is the heart of my purpose. You are a
gentleman of excellent breeding, admirable discourse, of great
admittance, authentic in your place and person, generally allow'd
for your many **war-like,** court-like, and learnèd preparations,—
FALSTAFF: O, sir!
FORD: Believe it, for you know it. There is money; spend it, spend
it; spend more; spend all I have; only give me so much of your
time in exchange for it, as to lay an amiable siege to the honesty
of this Ford's wife; use your art of wooing; win her to consent to
you; if any man may, you may as soon as any.
FALSTAFF: Would it apply well to the vehemency of your affection,

that I should win what you would enjoy? Methinks you prescribe to yourself very preposterously.

FORD: O, understand my drift. She dwells so securely on the excellency of her honour, that the folly of my soul dares not present itself; she is too bright to be look'd against. How could I come to her with any detection in my hand, my desires had instance and argument to commend themselves. I could drive her then from the ward of her purity, her reputation, her marriage-vow, and a thousand other her defences, which now are too-too strongly embattled against me.

What say you to 't, Sir John?

FALSTAFF: Master Brook, I will first make bold with your money; next give me your hand, at last, as I am a gentleman, you shall, if you will, enjoy Ford's wife.

The King himself spouts blood and fire in *King Henry V* (III, iii, 10–18):

> The gates of mercy shall be all shut up;
> And the flesh'd soldier – rough and hard of heart—
> In liberty of bloody hand shall range
> With conscience wide as Hell: mowing like grass
> Your fresh-fair virgins and your flowing infants;
> What is it then to me, if impious **war,**—
> Array'd in flames, like to the prince of fiends—
> Do, with his smirch'd complexion all fell feats
> Enlink'd to waste and desolation?

In *King Henry VIII* it is Cardinal Wolsey who gives phrase to the dire effects of total war (III, ii, 367–373):

> ... Oh, how wretched,
> Is that poor man that hangs on princes' favours!
> There is, betwixt that smile we would aspire to,
> That sweet aspect of princes, and their ruin,
> More pangs and fears than **wars** or women have:
> And when he falls, he falls like Lucifer,
> Never to hope again.

In *Julius Caesar* it is Mark Antony who best describes the havoc of war in a speech which, though every schoolboy may know it, cannot be evaded (III, 1, 263):

> A curse shall light upon the limbs of men;
> Domestic fury and fierce civil strife
> Shall cumber all the parts of Italy;
> Blood and destruction shall be so in use,
> And dreadful objects so familiar,
> That mothers shall but smile when they behold
> Their infants quarter'd with the hands of **war**;
> All pity chok'd with custom of fell deeds;
> And Caesar's spirit, ranging for revenge,
> With Atê by his side come hot from Hell,
> Shall in these confines with a monarch's voice
> Cry *Havoc*! and let slip the dogs of **war**;
> That this foul deed shall smell above the earth
> With carrion men, groaning for burial.

Much less well-known is a speech of Octavius Caesar in *Antony and Cleopatra* (IV, 1, 10–16), which concludes with a curious expression of sympathy for Mark Antony himself:

> —Let our best heads
> Know, that to-morrow the last of many battles
> We mean to fight. Within our files there are,
> Of those that served Mark Antony but late,
> Enough to fetch him in. See it be done:
> And feast the army; we have store to do't,
> And they have earn'd the waste. Poor Antony!

More tortuous still is the misanthropic hero of *Timon of Athens* (v, 1, 166–174) saying in good set terms what he thinks of the mad world's favourite pastime:

> If Alcibiades kill my countrymen
> Let Alcibiades know this of Timon,
> That Timon cares not. But, if he sack fair Athens,
> And take our goodly agêd men by th' beards,

Giving our holy virgins to the stain
Of contumelious, beastly, mad-brained **war,**
Then let him know – and tell him Timon speaks it
In pity of our agèd and our youth, –
I cannot choose but tell him that I care not,
And let him take't at worst; for their knives care not,
While you have throats to answer . . .

The unfortunate hero of *Titus Andronicus* buries two of his
sons (I, I, 89–95) who have been slain in the course of war:

Make way to lay them by their brethren –
                                    [*the tomb is opened*]
There greet in silence as the dead are wont,
And sleep in peace, slain in your country's **wars**!
O sacred receptacle of my joys,
Sweet cells of virtue and nobility,
How many sons of mine hast thou in store,
That thou wilt never render to me more!

Two of the dire ladies in *Troilus and Cressida* have dreams
of the 'bloody turbulence' of war (v, iii, 8–13):

CASSANDRA: Where is my brother Hector?
ANDROMACHE: Here, sister, arm'd and bloody in intent.
  Consort with me in loud and due petition,
  Pursue we him on knees; for I have dream'd
  Of bloody turbulence, and this whole night
  Hath nothing seen but shapes and forms of slaughter.
CASSANDRA: O, it is true.

In *The Merchant of Venice*, that popular drama written
around the subject of race-hatred, there is no actual bloodshed
though much talk of it in connection with the payment of
a bond. And perhaps the whole play's most ominous phrase,
'fit for treasons, stratagems, and spoils' (v, I, 85) is uttered
by the moonstruck Lorenzo as applicable to the sort of man
who has no time for music in his soul.

Nothing in the whole of *Macbeth*, that blood-boltered tragedy of ambition, is more frightening than this colloquy – eight words in all – between the tyrant and the first of his hired assassins (III, 4, 11–12):

> MACBETH: There's blood upon thy face
> FIRST MURDERER: 'Tis Banquo's then.

Othello, giving instructions to his lieutenant Iago after the brawl, also generalizes about peace and war in *Othello* (II, 3, 240–243) before going back to bed:

> Iago, look with care about the town,
> And silence those whom this vile brawl distracted—
> Come, Desdemona: 'tis the soldier's life
> To have their balmy slumbers waked with strife.

Edgar in the heart-aching tragedy of *King Lear* (III, 4, 76–78) has a snatch of a sinister song with the odour of blood in it:

> Child Roland to the dark tower came;
> His word was still, Fie, foh and fum,
> I smell the blood of a British man.

Fortinbras at the very end of *Hamlet* orders a ceremonial funeral for the play's dead hero (V, 2, 388–393):

> Let four captains
> Bear Hamlet, like a soldier, to the stage;
> For he was likely, had he been put on,
> T'have proved most royally; and, for his passage,
> The soldiers' music and the rites of **war**
> Speak loudly for him.—

Twenty lines of what is perhaps the oddest of all the comedies, *All's Well That Ends Well* (II, 3, 273) may be said to contain the whole play in its quiddity – the praise of war, of subtlety, and of infidelity and lack of faith:

[105]

PAROLLES: – To the **wars,** my boy, to the **wars**!
  He wears his honour in a box unseen,
  That hugs his kicky-wicky here at home,
  Spending his manly marrow in his arms,
  Which should sustain the bound and high curvet
  Of Mars's fiery steed. To other regions
  France is a stable, we that dwell in't jades.
  Therefore to the **war.**
BERTRAM: It shall be so. I'll send her to my house,
  Acquaint my mother with my hate to her,
  And wherefore I am fled . . . **war** is no strife
  To the dark house and the deserted wife
PAROLLES: Will this capriccio hold in thee, art sure?
BERTRAM: Go with me to my chamber, and advise me,
  I'll send her straight away; to-morrow
  I'll to the **wars,** she to her single sorrow.
PAROLLES: Why, these balls bound, there's noise in it. 'Tis hard:
  A young man married is a man that's marred:
  Therefore away, and leave her bravely: go . . .

In *Pericles, Prince of Tyre* the character called Boult whose lowest of professions is that of Servant to a Pander in a brothel, thinks he might be even worse off as a soldier in a war (IV, 5, 160–164):

> What would you have me do? go to the **wars,**
> would you? where a man may serve seven years
> for the loss of a leg, and have not money enough
> in the end to buy him a wooden one?

In another very odd play, *Measure for Measure,* another brothel-keeper argues that war is very bad for her business (I, 2, 75–77):

MISTRESS
OVERDONE: Thus, what with the **war,** what with the sweat, what with the gallows, and what with poverty, I am custom-shrunk.

Among the sweeter comedies, *As You Like It* has no note

of war at all, but only a contrasting note of peace from a peace-loving shepherd (III, 2, 67–71):

CORIN: Sir, I am a true labourer: I earn what I eat, get that I wear; owe no man hate, envy no man's happiness; glad of other men's good, content with my harm; and the greatest of my pride is to see my ewes graze and my lambs suck.

In *Twelfth Night* the only mention of war is a vague incidental rumble in the background (V, 1, 47–57):

VIOLA: Here comes the man, sir that did rescue me.
  [*Enter Officers with Antonio*]
DUKE: That face of his I do remember well.
  Yet when I saw it last, it was besmear'd
  As black as Vulcan in the smoke of **war**:
  A baubling vessel was he captain of,
  For shallow draught and bulk unprizable,
  With which such scathful grapple did he make
  With the most noble bottom of our fleet,
  That very envy and the tongue of loss
  Cried fame and honour on him . . .

In *Much Ado About Nothing* the witty young men are soldiers by profession, but soldiers on leave in sunny Sicily (I, 1, 43–54):

BEATRICE: I pray you, how many hath he kill'd and eaten in these **wars**? But how many hath he kill'd?
  For indeed, I promised to eat all of his killing.
LEONATA: Faith, niece, you tax Signor Benedick too much, but he'll be meet with you I doubt it not.
MESSENGER: He hath done good service, lady, in these **wars**.
BEATRICE: You had musty victual, and he hath help to eat it; he's a very valiant trencher-man; he hath an excellent stomach.
MESSENGER: And a good soldier too, lady.
BEATRICE: And a good soldier to a lady; but what is he to a lord?
MESSENGER: A lord to a lord, a man to a man; stuff'd with all honourable virtues.

BEATRICE: It is so, indeed; he is no less than a stuff'd man; but for the stuffing, – well, we are all mortal.

LEONATO: You must not, sir, mistake my niece. There is a kind of merry **war** betwixt Signor Benedick and her: they never meet but there's a skirmish of wit between them.

In the early farce, *The Two Gentlemen of Verona*, there is but a single and a flying reference to things martial (v, 2, 15–16):

THURIO: How likes she my discourse?

PROTEUS: Ill, when you talk of **war**.

THURIO: But well, when I discourse of love and peace?

JULIA [aside]: But, indeed, better when you hold your peace.

In the other early farce, *The Comedy of Errors*, the allusion is again a hind-sight reference (v, 1, 189–193):
Antipholus of Ephesus to the Duke thereof:

> Justice, most gracious Duke, O grant me justice!
> Even for the service that long since I did thee,
> When I bestrid thee in the **wars** and took
> Deep scars to save thy life; even for the blood
> That then I lost for thee, now grant me justice.

In *Love's Labour's Lost* (v, 2, 653) the fantastical Spaniard called Don Adriano has a comment on Hector the Trojan whose part he has to play in a masque at the end of the comedy itself (v, 2, 653). These striking words were very memorably spoken at Stratford-on-Avon by Paul Scofield in his early twenties:

> The sweet **war-man** is dead and rotten; sweet chuck,
> beat not the bones of the buried: when he breathed,
> he was a man.

Prospero in *The Tempest* sets the very elements at war with one another v, 1, 41–50):

> – I have bedimm'd
> The noontide sun, call'd forth the mutinous winds,
> And 'twixt the green sea and the azure'd vault
> Set roaring **war**: to the dread-rattling thunder
> Have I given fire, and rifted Jove's stout oak
> With his own bolt: the strong-based promontory
> Have I make shake, and by the spurs pluck'd up
> The pine and cedar: graves at my command
> Have waked their sleepers, oped, and let 'em forth
> By my so potent art.

The fantasy, *A Midsummer Night's Dream*, comes no nearer to war than a fairy wrangle between Oberon and Titania as to which should possess a little Indian boy. All the rest is misunderstanding and moonshine and magic, a ducal wedding and some bungled play-acting by artisans.

Mankind – whether making war or trying to maintain peace – is pleasantly rebuked by the sprite Puck (III, 2, 115) in the single line, 'Lord, what fools these mortals be.'

That necromancer among stage-directors, Mr Peter Brook, has recently and sensationally given the world – the whole world – a production of this play which is said to make it look like a supernatural circus. One shall hope to catch up with this at Omsk, or Ormskirk, or Oklahoma City.

INDEX OF QUOTATIONS

All's Well That Ends Well   105, 106
Antony and Cleopatra   12, 13, 15, 19, 25, 39–40, 47, 48–9, 53, 54, 57, 58–9, 63, 71, 103, 106–7
As You Like It   9, 16, 20, 32, 33, 34, 76, 82–3
The Comedy of Errors   108
Coriolanus   22, 61, 80–1
Cymbeline   10, 19, 29, 79, 85
Hamlet   16, 18, 23, 28, 37, 69, 105
King Henry IV, Part One   35–6, 61, 64, 72, 83–4, 100–1
King Henry IV, Part Two   21, 65–6, 71, 74, 77, 79, 101
King Henry V   9, 14, 18, 27, 29, 31, 35, 72, 87–9, 94–5, 102
King Henry VI, Part One   15, 29, 95–6
King Henry VI, Part Two   72, 75, 89, 96–7
King Henry VI, Part Three   25, 72, 97–8
King Henry VIII   66, 102
King John   25, 39, 62, 67, 99–100
Julius Caesar   46, 86, 103
King Lear   13, 24, 30–1, 34–5, 42, 72, 86, 105
Love's Labour's Lost   11, 22, 26, 66, 68, 108
Macbeth   33, 61, 89–92, 105
Measure for Measure   24, 37, 42, 106
The Merchant of Venice   46, 56, 60–1, 75, 84, 104
The Merry Wives of Windsor   30, 78, 101–2
A Midsummer Night's Dream   26, 40–1, 65, 70, 84–5, 109
Much Ado About Nothing   12, 32–3, 45, 68, 79, 83, 85, 107–8
Othello   15–16, 46, 57, 71, 93–4, 105
Pericles, Prince of Tyre   23–4, 58, 66, 73, 106
The Rape of Lucrece   46
King Richard II   21–2, 57, 62, 64, 73, 99

King Richard III   29–30, 66, 72, 98–9
Romeo and Juliet   15, 30, 37, 45, 84
The Taming of the Shrew   20, 25, 38, 39
The Tempest   41–2, 45, 65, 67, 71, 81–2, 86, 108–9
Timon of Athens   62, 103–4
Titus Andronicus   13–14, 20, 26, 104
Troilus and Cressida   72, 104
Twelfth Night   9, 17, 27, 32, 36, 37, 40, 57, 70, 73, 81, 107
The Two Gentlemen of Verona   58, 66, 79, 108
Venus and Adonis   21, 29, 43–4
The Winter's Tale   17, 31, 61, 74, 80